Volker Fischer

Richard Meier
Der Architekt als Designer und Künstler
The Architect as Designer and Artist

Volker Fischer

Richard Meier
Der Architekt als Designer und Künstler
The Architect as Designer and Artist

Edition Axel Menges

© 2003 Edition Axel Menges, Stuttgart/London
ISBN 3-932565-32-0 Buchhandelsausgabe/
Book-trade edition
ISBN 3-932565-34-7 Katalogausgabe/Catalogue
edition

Alle Rechte vorbehalten, besonders die der Übersetzung in andere Sprachen.
All rights reserved, especially those of translation into other languages.

Reproduktionen/Reproductions: Bild und Text Joachim Baun, Fellbach
Druck/Printing: Druckhaus Münster GmbH, Kornwestheim
Bindearbeiten/Binding: Postkonfekt GmbH, Seeheim-Jugenheim

Übersetzung ins Englische/Translation into English: Marion McClellan
Design: Axel Menges

Inhalt

6   Vorwort von James M. Bradburne

8   Ein emblematischer Enkel der Moderne.
    Eine Einführung

14 Objekte für Räume
30 Objekte für Tisch und Schreibtisch
52 Persönliche Accessoires
58 Collagen und Skulpturen

82 Das Museum für Angewandte Kunst in
    Frankfurt am Main

126 Anmerkungen
127 Danksagung
128 Abbildungsnachweis

Contents

7   Preface by James M. Bradburne

9   An emblematic grandson of Modernism.
    An introduction

15 Objects for rooms
31 Table tops and desktop accessories
53 Personal design
59 Collages and sculptures

83 The Museum for Applied Arts in Frankfurt
    am Main

126 Notes
127 Acknowledgement
128 Sources of illustrations

Vorwort

Einige Zeit nach der Eröffnung besuchte ich Richard Meiers Museum in Frankfurt am Main. Das war 1989, und ich war Student der Architectural Association School in London. Das exklusive, vornehme weiße Gebäude, exakt geplant und ausgeführt mit einer bemerkenswerten Präzision der Details, war damals ein leuchtendes, eindrucksvolles Beispiel für einen spätmodernen Klassizismus. Damals, als ich durch die lichtdurchfluteten Rampen und Räume wanderte, hätte ich nicht im Traum daran gedacht, zehn Jahre später als Direktor in dieses wunderbare Haus zurückzukehren.

Seit seiner Eröffnung im April 1985 hat dieses Museum von Richard Meier ebenso Bewunderung wie Kritik auf sich gezogen. Während Architekten und Museumsbesucher das Haus lieben, kritisieren es Museumsfachleute als zu lichtdurchflutet, zu unflexibel und bemängeln die starre Präsentation der Sammlungen. Sicherlich macht es die fest eingebaute Landschaft der Vitrinen, die dominant den Charakter des Gebäudes im Inneren bestimmt, schwierig, Änderungen der Präsentation vorzunehmen. Andere Kritiker stören sich daran, daß die Architektur des Gebäudes so dominant ist, daß die Sammlungsgegenstände marginalisiert werden würden.

Sowohl als Architekt wie als Museumsfachmann ist es seit langem meine Überzeugung, daß ein Museum ein öffentlicher Platz ist und daß seine Aktivitäten und Programme in gesellschaftlichen Kontexten gesehen und beurteilt werden sollten. Die Architektur eines Museums sollte zuallererst kommunikative Interaktionen fördern und unterstützen: als Grundlage für die Ausbildung von Fähigkeiten, mit Kultur angemessen umzugehen. 1980 bemerkte Nelson Goodman: »Ein Museum hat die Funktion, als Institution der Blindheit vorzubeugen, indem es seine Sammlungsgegenstände und Ausstellungsstücke zum Sprechen bringt. Und Werke zum Sprechen zu bringen, ist die wichtigste Aufgabe eines Museums. Werke sprechen dann, wenn sie intensivere Anschauung, genauere Wahrnehmung provozieren und visuelle Intelligenz, erweiterte Perspektiven freisetzen. Indem sie wichtige Aspekte, die vergessen oder unterdrückt sind, betonen, beteiligen sie sich an der Organisation und Reorganisation von Erfahrungen, an der Etablierung und dem Offenhalten unserer Weltsicht(en).« Als ich im Januar 1999 zum Direktor des Museums berufen wurde, war für mich die Richtung der notwendigen Veränderungen klar: das Museum auch inhaltlich so innovativ, dynamisch und international zu positionieren, wie das Gebäude von Richard Meier selbst es nahelegt, in dem die Sammlungen gezeigt werden.

Fünfzehn Jahre nach der Eröffnung des Museums am 10. Mai 2000, wurde das Museum mit neuen Inhalten, Präsentationsformen und erweiterten Aufgaben »wiedereröffnet« und bekam einen neuen Namen: »mak.frankfurt« (Museum für Angewandte Kunst). Das Museum wurde zu einer »piazza«, einem öffentlichen Ort der Begegnung für unterschiedliche Besucher und Benutzergruppen. Ein Ort für informelles Lernen, ein Ort für Experimente und Innovationen, also ein Ort, der das Museum im 21. Jahrhundert positioniert und verankert. Um diese Veränderungen voranzutreiben, besuchte ich Richard Meier 1999 in New York und besprach mit ihm die notwendigen architektonischen Eingriffe für diese Neupositionierung. Das betraf Veränderungen der fest eingebauten Vitrinen, zusätzliche Lichtkontrollen in den Ausstellungsräumen, neue Präsentationselemente wie Lesetische, tragbare, leichte Sitzhocker und fest an den Vitrinen verankerte Leitern, um auch kleinen Museumsbesuchern Blicke auf die Objekte zu ermöglichen. Ebenso sprachen wir über die Neugestaltung und Erweiterung des Museumscafés. Zusätzlich zu diesen vorgeschlagenen Veränderungen schuf Richard Meier dankenswerterweise eine neue Oberflächenstruktur für den offenen Innenhof des Museums. Nun präsentiert sich dieser Hof als »Steingarten« mit wellenartigen Höhenunterschieden, weil der bis dahin angepflanzte Bodendecker aus Efeu aufgrund fehlender Lichteinstrahlung den Boden nur partiell abdeckte.

Das Ergebnis unserer Zusammenarbeit markiert den gegenwärtigen Zustand des Hauses und der Institution. Der Bau und die Institution sind dialektische Partner und beziehen die Besucher in diese Dialektik mit ein. Alle Wandtexte des Museums sind auf farbigen Fonds sowohl in Deutsch wie in Englisch ausgeführt, und unser Haus ist das einzige Museum in Deutschland mit türkischen und arabischen Wandtexten. Auf jedem Geschoß gibt es Lesetische sowie das Angebot, das Internet zu nutzen. Inzwischen präsentiert das Museum eine ständige Design-Sammlung sowie eine Sammlung digitaler Gegenstände, die wir als angewandte Kunst des 21. Jahrhunderts verstehen (wir nennen dieses Sammlungs- und Forschungsfeld »Digital Craft«). Im Mai 2002 zeigte das Museum die Ausstellung »I love you« und thematisierte damit Computerviren als legitimes Feld angewandter Kunst!

Im gesamten Museum sind Workshop-Räume, Computer-Labore und Leseecken verteilt. Der Museumsshop »mak 3«, einer der qualitätvollsten Museumsshops in Deutschland, verknüpft die Sammlungen und Ausstellungen des Museums mit Kaufmöglichkeiten für die Besucher, denn viele der angebotenen Objekte finden sich in den Ausstellungsräumen wieder. Auch das Museumsrestaurant ist sehr erfolgreich. Unser Restaurant »Emma Metzler« wird inzwischen als eine der besten gastronomischen Adressen der Stadt gehandelt, und die Neueinrichtung des Cafés beinhaltet auch regelmäßig wechselnde Präsentationen von Sammlungs- und Sonderausstellungsobjekten.

Eine überraschende Konsequenz der erneuten Zusammenarbeit mit Richard Meier war für mich die Entdeckung seiner vielfältigen anderen kreativen Talente. Sein Werk als Architekt ist international hoch geschätzt: 1984 erhielt er den Pritzker-Preis. Nun erschloß sich mir Meier als ein profunder Produktdesigner, Möbelentwerfer und bildender Künstler. Sicherlich kannte ich viele seiner Produkte – unsere Design-Abteilung zeigt einige seiner Entwürfe für das amerikanische Unternehmen Swid Powell –, und einige seiner Möbel sind ebenso Teil unserer Sammlung. Um so mehr war ich überrascht über die Intensität und Vielfältigkeit seines bildnerischen Werkes, über die Collagen, Skulpturen und Zeichnungen.

Ein Museum ist mehr als nur ein Gebäude: es ist eine lebendige und wachsende Institution. Jedes Museum und jede Ausstellung schuldet insofern jenen Personen tiefen Dank, die diese Lebendigkeit, diese Kommunikativität ermöglichen und fördern. Nicht alle, denen unser Haus in dieser Hinsicht Dank schuldet, kann ich erwähnen, aber doch und gerade diejenigen, die die Ausstellung und die begleitende Publikation unterstützt haben:

die Frankfurter Privatbank Hauck & Aufhäuser, die generell die Aktivitäten und Ausstellungen des Museums seit Jahren großzügig fördert;

die Messe Frankfurt, die uns über viele Jahre hinweg inzwischen ein ebenso zuverlässiger wie generöser Partner ist und ermöglicht hat, daß zeitgenössisches Design im Museum eine permanente Heimstatt hat;

Volker Fischer, der seit zehn Jahren der Produktgestaltung eine prominente Rolle im Museum ermöglicht und erarbeitet hat;

Richard Meier für seine solidarische, aber auch visionäre Unterstützung unserer Weiterentwicklungen. Ohne ihn wäre unser Museum nicht der faszinierende Ort, der er zweifellos ist und in der Zukunft bleiben wird.

James M. Bradburne

Preface

I first visited Richard's Meier's museum in Frankfurt soon after it was opened. The year was 1989, and I was a student of architecture at the Architectural Association in London. The pristine white building, rigorously planned and executed with painstaking attention to detail, was a shining example of Late-Modern classicism. I certainly never suspected as I wandered through the serene light-filled volumes of the museum, that in ten years time I would have the pleasure of being its director.

Since it was opened in April 1985, Meier's museum building – his first – has attracted criticism as well as praise. Loved by architects and the public alike, many museum professionals complained that it was unusable as a museum – it was too light, too inflexible, too sparsely inhabited by its collections. Certainly the built in landscape of showcases – one of the outstanding features of the museum – makes it a challenge to change the museum's displays. Others argued that the museum's architecture overwhelmed the museum's objects, making the building an architectural monologue.

It has long been my conviction – as both an architect and a museum professional – that the museum is a public space, and the museum's effectiveness – and that of its architecture – must be understood in social terms. The museum's architecture, while it serves other masters, must first and foremost contribute to and support the social interaction that is the foundation of the skills of appropriating culture. Nelson Goodman noticed in 1980: »The museum has to function as an institution for the prevention of blindness in order to make works work. And making works work is the museum's major mission. Works work when, by stimulating inquisitive looking, sharpening perception, raising visual intelligence, widening perspectives and marking off neglected significant kinds, they participate in the organisation and reorganisation of experience, in the making and re-making of our worlds.« When I became Director of the museum in January 1999, the challenge was clear – to make the museum as innovative, dynamic and international as the Richard Meier building that housed its collections.

On 10 May 2000, fifteen years after the Meier building was opened, the museum was relaunched with a new name – mak.frankfurt (the Museum for Applied Arts) – and a broadened mission. The museum was to become a public »piazza«, open to a broad public. It was to be a site for informal learning and a site for experiments and innovation in what a museum could and should be – a »museum for the 21st century«. To realise this step forward, I visited Richard Meier in New York in 1999 to discuss the architectural implications of the relaunch. These included altering the original showcase landscape, introducing additional light control measures, designing new display elements such as reading tables, portable stools, and ladders for children to see into tall showcases – as well as the refurbishment and enlargement of the museum café. In addition to reviewing the proposed changes, Richard Meier generously redesigned the museum's courtyard as a »stone garden« of undulating gravel waves – a vast improvement over the original planting which had suffered over the years for lack of direct sunlight.

The consequence of this collaboration can be seen today at mak.frankfurt. The museum and the building are partners in a dialogue that includes the museum visitor. The wall texts throughout the museum are in German and English on a coloured background, and mak.frankfurt is the only museum in Germany with texts in Turkish and Arabic. There are reading tables on every floor and wireless Internet access throughout the museum. The museum now has a permanent collection of contemporary design and one of the world's only permanent collections of the applied art of the 21st century (so-called »Digital Craft«) – websites, computer games, and emulators. In May 2002, the museum hosted the exhibition »I love you« – featuring the computer virus as applied art!

Throughout the museum there are workshops, computer labs, and reading corners. The museum shop mak.3 is one of the best of its kind, linking the museum's collections and exhibitions to the visitor by offering objects selected for the museum's collections for sale. The restaurant too is flourishing. The restaurant »Emma Metzler« is already recognised as one of Frankfurt's best, and the newly designed interior also features regularly changing displays of objects drawn from the museum's own collections.

One of the other happy consequences of this process was discovering the many-sided talent of Richard Meier. Internationally recognised for his work as an architect (he was awarded the Pritzker Prize in 1984), I discovered that Meier is also a gifted product designer, furniture designer, and artist. I knew of Meier's work as a designer, of course, and the museum's collections include several of the pieces he designed for Swid Powell, as well as some of his best known furniture. On the other hand, I was struck by the richness and intensity of Richard Meier's work as an artist – collages, sculptures, drawings all figure in Richard Meier's remarkable output.

A museum is not only its building, but a living and growing institution. Every museum and every museum exhibition owes countless debts of gratitude to those who make it a vital and lively public space, of which only a few of them can be mentioned due to lack of space. I would personally like to thank:

the Bankhaus Hauck & Aufhäuser for their generous support of the museum and its exhibitions over the past years;

the Messe Frankfurt for its longstanding partnership with the museum to ensures that design has a permanent home in Frankfurt;

Volker Fischer, who has spent the last decade putting design at the forefront of the museum's activities;

Richard Meier, for his all-embracing vision and his openness to change, without which the museum would not be the place – in the fullest sense of the word – it is and will continue to be in the future.

James M. Bradburne

Ein emblematischer Enkel der Moderne. Eine Einführung

Dieses Buch und die begleitende Ausstellung widmen sich einem Gestalter, der die Reichhaltigkeit und die Entdeckungen, die Versprechungen und Abenteuer der Vergangenheit schätzt und liebt: vor allem jene der klassischen Moderne, also der Wiener Schule, des De Stijl, des russischen Konstruktivismus und der Bauhaus-Moderne. Aber Richard Meier goutiert nicht nur den Charakter und die Schönheiten dieser Jahrzehnte, sondern verwandelt sie eigenschöpferisch. Wenn sich ein so außergewöhnliches Talent wie dieser Entwerfer an so außergewöhnlichen Talenten wie Frank Lloyd Wright, Otto Wagner, Josef Hoffmann, Charles Rennie Mackintosh, Gerrit Rietveld, Kasimir Malewitsch oder Le Corbusier reibt, dann ergibt diese Reibung etwas aufregend Neues, dem das Alte als anregende Erinnerung eingeschrieben ist. Das ist mehr postmodern als modern gedacht und eher darauf aus, genetisch aus dem Alten das Neue zu kreieren, als das Neue für absolut zu setzen; eine subkutane Arroganz im übrigen, mit der die Moderne trotz all ihrer rhetorischen Heroik der permanenten Neuerungen immer ihre Legitimationsprobleme hatte.

Richard Meier arbeitet als Gestalter – als Architekt, Designer und Künstler –, also an einer umfassenden »Revision der Moderne« der Zeit zwischen 1890 und 1930. Dabei interessieren ihn die ästhetischen Visionen dieser so produktiven Jahrzehnte weit mehr als die sozialen Implikationen, die mit ihnen verbunden waren. Insofern hat er mit den gesellschaftspolitischen, in den Worten von Jürgen Habermas »unabgegoltenen Versprechen der Moderne« nichts oder kaum etwas im Sinn. Aber sich auf die Ästhetik der europäischen Moderne zu konzentrieren, scheint bei ihm gleichzeitig auch eine gewisse Aversion zu bedeuten: gegen die Zumutungen einer trivialisierten amerikanischen Alltagskultur; gegen eine, nicht nur ästhetische, Traditionsvergeßlichkeit, die allenfalls in den Versandhauskatalogen amerikanischer Kaufhäuser Pseudostile wie »Edwardian Club«, »Gothic Revival« oder »Chippendale Colonial« als zugleich hilflose wie kitschige Melangen ehemaliger Originalität offerieren. Anderseits hat ein Zeitgenosse Richard Meiers, der amerikanische Architekt Robert Venturi, genau dies zu seinem ästhetischen Programm gemacht, also die Alltagskultur und den Kitsch, aber beides dann durchaus gestalterisch veredelt. Andere architektonische Weggefährten Meiers wie etwa Frank Gehry haben sich entweder in die Delirien computergenerierter, dekonstruktivistischer Entwurfsprozesse gestürzt oder wie Stanley Tigerman den Hollywood-Pop ironisch überhöht. Meier ist da wesentlich beharrender, auch »europäischer«. Er ist gewissermaßen aktiv »auf der Suche nach der verlorenen Zeit«, vergleichbar allenfalls dem italienischen Architekten Paolo Porthogesi, der sich allerdings mit seinen Produkten fast immer in den Manierismen des Manierismus verliert. Meier dagegen kann eher mit der »Belle Epoque« um 1890 etwas anfangen. Nicht zufällig sind seine Wettbewerbsisometrien oft, z. B. für das Museum für Kunsthandwerk in Frankfurt am Main (heute: Museum für Angewandte Kunst), mit Staffagefiguren von Otto Wagner bevölkert, was Meiers strahlend weißer, stereometrischer Moderne geradezu etwas Nostalgisches gibt.[1]

Richard Meier, 1935 geboren, war von 1970 bis 1976 Mitglied jener berühmten New Yorker Architektengruppe »The New York Five«, die sich die Fortschreibung und Erneuerung paradigmatischer Prinzipien der klassischen europäischen Moderne der 1920er Jahre verschrieben hatte und deshalb unter dem Begriff »The Whites« bekannt wurde. Weitere Mitstreiter dieser Gruppe waren damals Michael Graves, Peter Eisenman, John Hejduk und Charles Gwathmey. Im programmatischen Gegensatz zu dieser Haltung formierten sich zur gleichen Zeit um die Architekten Robert Venturi und Robert A. M. Stern die sogenannten »Greys« – Gestalter, die in ihrer Arbeit die hybriden Kulturidiome des amerikanischen Alltags, auch Kitsch und Pop, zum Ausgangspunkt ihrer Überlegungen machten. Wenn Venturi statuierte: »Mainstreet is almost alright« und damit die Abfolge banaler, gewöhnlicher Bauten legitimierte, antwortete Meier mit dem Verweis auf die verlorengegangene Heroik der »weißen Moderne«, die es gegen alle Zumutungen der Gegenwart zu bewahren gelte. Beide Gruppen trugen ihre theoretischen Debatten in der einflußreichen amerikanischen Architekturzeitschrift *Oppositions* aus und bestimmten damit in Theorie und Praxis den inhaltlichen Architekturdiskurs in den Vereinigten Staaten für gut ein Jahrzehnt.

Richard Meier wurde zunächst mit programmatischen Privathäusern (Saltzman House, East Hampton, New York, 1967–69; Douglas House, Harbor Springs, Michigan, 1971–73) bekannt, die, auf großen, freien, üppig begrünten Grundstücken errichtet, Raum- und Kubaturvorstellungen von Le Corbusier und Louis Kahn, in eingeschränkterem Maße auch von Ludwig Mies van der Rohe und Hans Scharoun, überblendeten und doch jeweils ein eigenständiges neues ästhetisches Ganzes ergaben. In seiner weiteren architektonischen Laufbahn ist Le Corbusier als Ausgangspotential Meiers wichtigster Referenzrahmen geblieben, zunehmend ergänzt durch Rekurse auf die Wiener Schule der Jahrhundertwende um 1900 und vor allem deren Protagonisten Josef Hoffmann, Adolf Loos, Otto Wagner. Der Kunstkritiker des Magazins *Time*, Robert Hughes, bemerkte: »Wenn irgendein Architekt ... mit eindeutiger Überzeugung die Absicht vertritt, das klassische Erbe der frühen Moderne (aber ohne deren Rhetorik der ›Wohnmaschine‹) zu erhalten, so ist dies Meier.«[2]

Am Ende der 1970er Jahre erhielt Meier mit dem Atheneum in New Harmony, Indiana, dem Museum für Kunsthandwerk in Frankfurt am Main und dem High Museum of Art in Atlanta, Georgia, jene Aufträge, die ihm dann internationale Reputation einbrachten. Alle diese Museen sind auf weitläufigen, parkähnlichen Grundstücken mit altem Baumbestand situiert und zeigen in ihren Grundrißdispositionen, den Verschmelzungen einander durchdringender Raumvolumen, dem luxuriösen Umgang mit der Mischung von Kunst- und Tageslicht sowie der Verwendung von Raumscheiben, Durchblicken, Verschneidungen, Emporen, Brücken und immer wieder Rampen, die das Raumkontinuum in steter Bewegung erschließen, sowie einer extensiven Bevorzugung der Farbe Weiß eine architek-

1. Richard Meier, Douglas House, Harbor Springs, Michigan, 1971–73.
2. Richard Meier, The Atheneum, New Harmony, Indiana, 1975–79.

**An emblematic grandson of Modernism.
An Introduction**

This book and the accompanying exhibition are devoted to a designer who values and loves the rich diversity, the promises, and the adventures of the past, above all the concepts of classical Modernism, the Viennese School, De Stijl, Russian Constructivism, and the Bauhaus Modernism. Richard Meier, however, not only delights in the character and beauty of these decades, but rather creatively adapts them to his own ideas. Whenever such an outstanding talent like this designer attempts to come to terms with such outstanding talents like Frank Lloyd Wright, Otto Wagner, Josef Hoffmann, Charles Rennie Macintosh, Gerrit Rietveld, Kasimir Malevitsch, or Le Corbusier, then this tension generates something new and exciting which creatively incorporates the old into its own memory. This is a Postmodern rather than a Modernist thought, and it aims to create something genetically novel from the traditional rather than laying claims to the new as something absolute. Besides, such a claim represents a subcutaneous arrogance which has created ongoing problems to Modernism by trying to become legitimate, in spite of the rhetorical heroism of its permanent innovations.

Richard Meier works as a formative creator – as an architect, designer, and artist – on an all-encompassing »revision of Modernism« of 1890 to 1930. In this endeavor, he is rather interested in the esthetic visions of those so very productive decades than in the social implications which are connected with them. In this respect, he has little or no use for the socio-political and – according to the words of Jürgen Habermas – »unsettled promises of Modernism«. By concentrating on the esthetics of European Modernism, however, he also seems to demonstrate his aversion to the impositions of a trivialized everyday American culture; to its forgetfulness of traditions, not only in the field of esthetics, which, at best, are offered in mail-order catalogues of American department stores as pseudo-styles like »Edwardian Club«, »Gothic Revival«, or »Chippendale Colonial«, which, in fact, represent a rather hapless and kitschy mélange of the original styles. On the other hand, a contemporary of Richard Meier's, the American architect Robert Venturi has used exactly this area, i.e. everyday culture and kitsch for his own esthetic program, but at the same time, he has generally elevated them in his artistic designs. Other architectural collegues of Richard Meier's, e.g. Frank Gehry, have either descended into the delirious depths of computer-generated Deconstructivist processes in designing or they have ironically over-elevated Hollywood Pop as Stanley Tigerman. Here, Meier is essentially more traditional, more »European«. In a certain sense, he is »searching for the lost past«, maybe comparable with the Italian architect Paolo Portoghesi who keeps losing himself in the manners of Mannerism. Meier, on the other hand, prefers the ideas of the »Belle Epoque« around 1890. It is not by accident that his isometrical competition drawings are frequently populated with staffage figures by Otto Wagner, e.g. for the Museum für Kunsthandwerk in Frankfurt am Main (today the Museum für Angewandte Kunst) rendering Meier's white, bright stereometrical Modernism almost nostalgic.[1]

From 1970 to 1976 Richard Meier, who was born in 1935, was a member of that famous New York group of architects called »The New York Five« whose goal was to continue and renew the paradigmatic principles of the classical European Modernism of the 1920's. They were therefore generally recognized as »The Whites«. At that time, other co-workers and co-fighters of this group were Michael Graves, Peter Eisenman, John Hejduk, and Charles Gwathmey. A contrasting program to this direction also formed during those days in the circle of the architects Robert Venturi and Robert A. M. Stern, the so-called »Greys« – designers whose work used the hybrid cultural idioms of American day-to-day life as starting points of their new artistic direction including kitsch and Pop. When Venturi stated that »Mainstreet is almost alright« and thus legitimized the rows of banal, commonplace edifices, Richard Meier responded by referring to the lost heroism of »white Modernism« which ought to be retained in spite of the unsensible demands of the present. The two groups fought their battles of ideas and theories in the influential architectural magazine *Oppositions* and thus determined theoretically and practically the contents of the architectural discourse in the United States for an entire decade.

Richard Meier first became acquainted with programmatic private houses (Saltzman House, East Hampton, New York, 1967–69; Douglas House, Harbor Springs, Michigan, 1971–73). They were situated on large, open, and verdant parklands and connected the ideas of space and

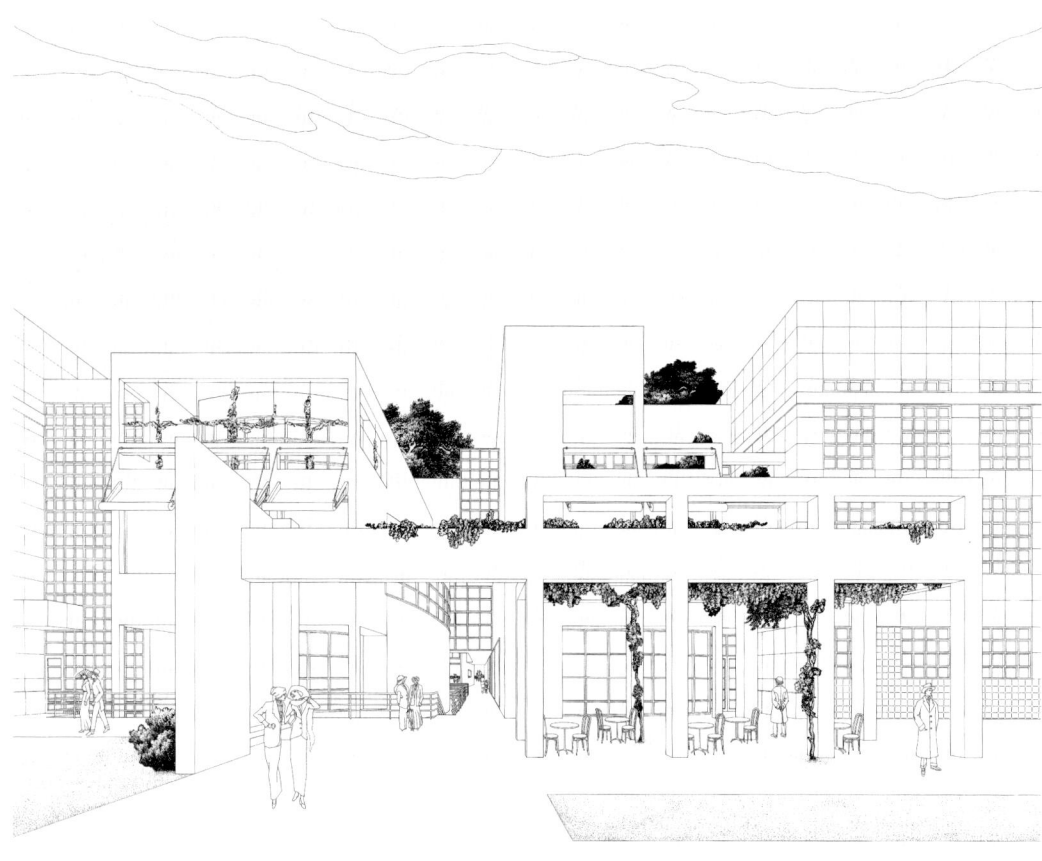

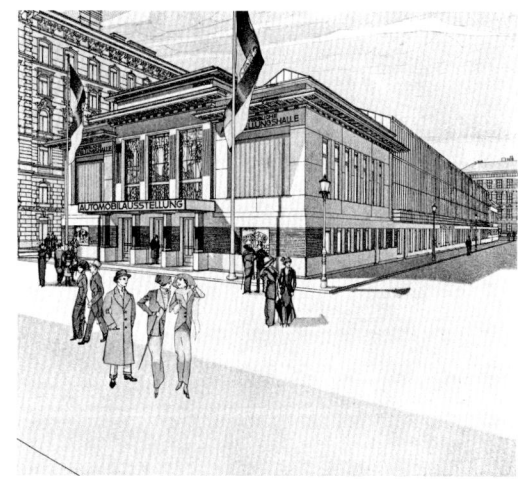

3. Richard Meier, Museum für Angewandte Kunst, Frankfurt am Main, 1979–85. Wettbewerbsentwurf, 1979.
4. Otto Wagner, Zedlitzhalle, Wien, zweites Projekt, 1913.
5. Le Corbusier, Villa Savoye, Poissy, 1929–31.

3. Richard Meier, Museum for Applied Arts, Frankfurt am Main, 1979–85. Competition project, 1979.
4. Otto Wagner, Zedlitzhalle, Wien, second project, 1913.
5. Le Corbusier, Villa Savoye, Poissy, 1929–31.

tonisch virtuos eingesetzte Matrix baukünstlerischer Perfektion. Dies führt – darin neben Le Corbusier auch den Raumerfindungen des russischen Konstruktivismus und des holländischen De Stijl verpflichtet – fast störrisch eine künstlerische Autonomie des Gebauten vor, der sich die pragmatischen Zwecke und Nutzungen unterzuordnen haben. Die vielleicht deutlichste Formulierung für diesen Autonomieanspruch hat Meier selbst einmal in einem Interview angesprochen: »The theme of my architecture is architecture.« Und an anderer Stelle sagt er über Architektur, sie sei »... primär ein Ausdrucksmittel für Meinungen, ein Wachhalten der Erinnerung. Im günstigsten Fall kann dies einmünden in eine Architektur reicher Collagen, komplexer Schichtungen und metaphorischer Bilder«.[3] Verschiedenartigste Bauaufgaben sind für ihn nicht mehr, aber auch nicht weniger als selbstreferentielle Variationen in einem komplexen Kosmos baukünstlerischer Strukturen und Systeme. Gleichwohl greifen da durchaus nicht die immer wieder geäußerten Bedenken vom »l'art pour l'art«, denn Meier hat die Nutzungsbriefings für seine Bauten, die sogenannten »Raumbücher«, immer äußerst genau eingehalten und bedient. Ein solcher Autonomieanspruch setzt voraus, auch vor der Innenausstattung der Lobbys und Fachbibliotheken, den festen Ausstellungsvitrinen und Display-Landschaften nicht Halt zu machen, sondern sie in einer Art Maßstabssprung aus der Matrix der Architektur wie Mikro-Architekturen fortzuschreiben. Bereits damit ist gesagt, daß Meier aus dieser Entwurfslogik heraus früher oder später auch die Ebene der Produkte gestalterisch in Angriff nehmen würde: Mobiliar, Porzellan, Glas und Silber für den gedeckten Tisch, Schreibtischutensilien, Leuchten, Schmuck, Uhren und Stoffe. Sein architektonisches Vokabular mit der eindeutigen Bevorzugung der Farbe Weiß im Äußeren wie im Inneren und den beschriebenen räumlichen Besonderheiten war in diesen Museumskomplexen fast lexikalisch definiert: eine Sprache, die er in der Folge bei zahlreichen weiteren Museen und Kulturgebäuden, ob in Barcelona, Ulm, München, Paris oder Den Haag, immer wieder anwendete, jeweils variiert und dem Genius loci angepaßt. Der Höhepunkt dieser definierten architektonischen Sprache war für den inzwischen 1984 als jüngster Preisträger mit dem Pritzker-Preis ausgezeichneten Architekten der Auftrag für das neue J. Paul Getty Center in Los Angeles, eine veritable neue »Akropolis«, eine Stadtkrone für diese kalifornische Kommune mit mehr als 20 Gebäuden, Gärten und internen Plätzen, bei der Meier seine architektonischen Überzeugungen in geradezu mikro-urbanistische Dimensionen erweitern konnte. In einer Planungs- und Bauzeit von mehr als zehn Jahren (1985–97) ist in Los Angeles ein Komplex entstanden, dessen Gesamtbausumme 1000 Millionen Dollar betrug. Damit handelte es sich um den größten Bauauftrag weltweit an einen freiberuflichen Architekten im 20. Jahrhundert.

Um so spannender ist es, die Dimensionen einmal umzukehren und im Detail aufzublättern, wie einer der erfolgreichsten Architekten der Welt mit den »kleinen Maßstäben« im Produktdesign umgeht, sowie zu sehen, daß dieser Architekt auch als bildender Künstler arbeitet, zweidimensional in Form von Collagen, dreidimensional in Form von Skulpturen. Während Meiers Architektur extensiv publiziert wurde und in ihrer Wiedererkennbarkeit einen allgemein bekannten Markstein heutigen Bauens darstellt, sind seine Produkte, Bildwerke und Plastiken weit weniger bekannt und publiziert.

Der englische Architekturkritiker Charles Jencks hat Richard Meier als »spätmodern« charakterisiert. Unabhängig davon, daß solche

cubature of Le Corbusier and Louis Kahn and, to a lesser degree also of Mies van der Rohe and Hans Scharoun, but each still presented an individual and new esthetic overall image. In Meier's continuing architectural development, Le Corbusier remained the most important point of reference and instigator. This was increasingly enriched through his recourse to the ideas of the Viennese School of the turn of the century around 1900 and especially to its protagonists Josef Hoffmann, Adolf Loos, and Otto Wagner. The art critic of the *Time* magazine, Robert Hughes, remarked: »If any architect ... represents, with undiluted conviction, the wish to preserve the classical legacy of twenties Modernism (but without its ›machine for livinging-in‹ rethoric) that person is Meier.«[2]

By the end of the 1970's, Meier received those new project offers, from the Atheneum in New Harmony, Indiana, the Museum für Kunsthandwerk in Frankfurt am Main, and the High Museum of Art in Atlanta, Georgia, which finally established his international reputation. All of these museums are situated within large expanses of parklands with mature trees. In their basic layout, the convergence of interrelated spaces, the luxuriously mixture of artificial and natural light, the use of space segments, special vistas, cross-overs, elevated levels, bridges, and ever-recurring ramps which let the spacial continuum appear in constant flux, as well as with the intense preference of the color white they present an ingeniously applied matrix of architectural perfection. Next to the ideas of Le Corbusier, this concept is also indebted to the spatial inventions of Russian Constructivism and the Dutch De Stijl movement and almost sternly dictates an artistic autonomy of structure to which any pragmatic use and application have to become subordinate. Possibly his clearest demand for this autonomy Meier once outlined in an interview with the words: »The theme of my architecture is architecture.« And in another context he says about architecture that it is »... primarily a means of expressing opinions and of a keeping awake the memories. At best, these ideas can merge with an architectural concept of rich collages, of complex structural layers, and of metaphorical images.«[3] The most diverse building jobs for him are no more and also no less than self-referencing variations in a complex cosmos of artistic structures and systems. Nevertheless, the occasionally voiced references to »l'art pour l'art« do not apply here, since Meier has always followed and executed with great attention to detail the users' briefings of his buildings.Such a demand for architectural autonomy does not expect to stop, not even at the internal furnishings in lobbies and special libraries or at the fixed showcases and display landscapes. It rather wants to be continued in a scale leap from the architectural matrix like a micro-architecture. This already anticipates that Meier sooner or later would transfer the application of his logic of design to the area of other products: furnishings, china, glass, and table silver, utensils for the writing desk, lights, jewelry, watches, and textiles. His architectural vocabulary with a definite preference of the color white for the exterior and down to the interior of the described spatial peculiarities was defined with almost lexical precision for these museums: a language which he applied in a sequence of numerous further projects of museums and cultural edifices, be it in Barcelona, Ulm, Munich, Paris, or The Hague, a language which he each time varies and adapts according to the individual genius loci. The high point of this defined architectural language came for Meier, who was honored in 1984 as the youngest winner of the Pritzker Prize, when he was awarded the project for the new J. Paul Getty Center in Los Angeles. This construction represented a veritable new »Acropolis« or crown of the city for this Californian community encompassing more than twenty buildings, gardens, and internal plazas. Here Meier was able to extend his architectural convictions almost down to micro-urbanistic dimensions. Over the planning and construction time of more than ten years (1985–97), a building complex was erected in Los Angeles, whose total cost reached 1000 million dollars. This meant that it was the largest construction contract given to any self-employed architect worldwide in the 20th century.

The matter becomes the more interesting, if we reverse the dimensions for a while in order to delineate how exactly one of the most successful architects of the world deals with the »small scales« of product design, as well as to understand that this architect also works as a design-

»Schubladen«-Klassifizierungen den tatsächlichen Variantenreichtum eines gestalterischen Œuvres ähnlich unzutreffend verallgemeinern wie die klassischen Stilbegriffe ganze Epochen, umreißt dieser Begriff doch einige dominante Überzeugungen und Entwurfshorizonte dieses Entwerfers. Zunächst fokussiert diese Bezeichnung jene leicht nostalgische Haltung des Architekten, der in der klassischen Moderne des ersten Viertels des 20. Jahrhunderts seine stärksten Anregungspotentiale aufspürt, dann betont das Präfix »spät« jenes charakteristische Herausfallen aus den üblichen zeitgenössischen Architektur-»Handschriften« etwa der Postmoderne, des Minimalismus und des Dekonstruktivismus, denen Meier überwiegend kritische Distanz entgegenbringt; und schließlich betont der Begriff auch dessen Konzentration auf die abgehobenen ästhetischen Substrate der Moderne und Neuen Sachlichkeit, da der gesellschaftliche und kulturelle Kontext heute ein völlig anderer ist als um 1900 oder 1920. Diese Kontextverschiebung hat prinzipiell etwas Vergleichbares zur Ontologie von Museen, die ihre Exponate zwangsläufig immer aus ihren Entstehungs- und Gebrauchsbedingungen herauslösen. Insofern hat es eine geradezu innere Evidenz, daß Richard Meier seit ca. 30 Jahren zu den erfolgreichsten Baumeistern heutiger Museen zählt. Und nicht zuletzt evoziert der Begriff »spätmodern« auch eine manieristische Spätphase einer Moderne, deren »klassische Zeit« unwiederbringlich vorüber ist. Die biologistische Geschichtsphilosophie Oswald Spenglers, der Kulturen als Organismen beschrieb, die prinzipiell dem Zyklus von Blüte, Reife und Verfall unterlägen, mag dabei eine Rolle gespielt haben, vielleicht auch das epochale kunsthistorische Buch über den Manierismus, welches Gustav René Hocke 1957 publizierte. Hocke beschreibt den Manierismus als Spätstil der Renaissance.[4] Daß Meier mit einer gewissen Berechtigung durchaus als »Manierist der Moderne« gelten kann, ist immer wieder geschrieben worden. Es geht um Feinheiten, Sensibilisierungen, Luxuriertheiten im gestalterischen Idiom, welche die »klassische Phase« der Moderne so nicht hatte, wohl auch nicht haben konnte und wollte. Und jene Haltung mag nur mit dem prinzipiellen Abstand einer amerikanischen Architektensozialisation der Ostküste der USA erklärbar sein, welche die europäische Geschichte der Moderne nicht zuletzt durch den Filter des von Philip Johnson propagierten »International Style« rezipieren mußte, vielleicht aber auch durch Meiers zeitweise Mitarbeit im Büro des nach New York emigrierten Bauhäuslers Marcel Breuer. Jene Denkfigur des »good old Europe«, die die sozialen Verwerfungen der Weimarer Republik und ihres gewaltsamen Endes im Nationalsozialismus sowie die sozial-utopischen Begründungs- und Erwartungshorizonte jener Republik zugunsten einer befriedeten, lediglich dominant ästhetischen Erfahrung verdichtet und gleichzeitig exkulpiert, hat auch Meiers Verständnis der europäischen Traditionen geprägt. Um nicht mißverstanden zu werden: Dies ist die Beschreibung einer Haltung, nicht deren Kritik. Denn die künstlerischen Ergebnisse dieser Haltung sind brillant im doppelten Sinne des Wortes: intellektuell und ästhetisch. Vielleicht aber ist ein dezidiert kulturpolitischer Verständnishorizont jenem Stilbegriff »spätmodern« am angemessensten. Denn Meier hat mit seiner an der »weißen Moderne« orientierten Architektursprache etwas nach Europa, speziell Deutschland, zurückgebracht, was die Nationalsozialisten jäh abgeschnitten hatten, verfemten, vertrieben, verfolgten. Auf das Museum für Angewandte Kunst in Frankfurt, seinen ersten in Europa realisierten Bau, bezogen, erinnert sich Meier noch heute: »Bei der Eröffnung sprach ich darüber, wie wichtig dieses Gebäude für mich war – als Amerikaner, als Architekt und als Jude. Ich konnte so helfen, eine Verbindung herzustellen zwischen der Gegenwart und dem, was im zweiten Weltkrieg zerstört worden war.«[5] In der Tat: Meier hat Deutschland, hat Europa etwas zurückgegeben – verändert, aktualisiert, neu interpretiert –, was verschüttet schien, erledigt, vertrieben, ausgerottet. Insofern tritt neben die ästhetische Brillanz die kulturpolitische Brisanz. Auf einer solchen Ebene ist Meiers »Spätmoderne« sehr wohl politisch, greift ein in die Befindlichkeiten des heutigen Europas, bezieht Position und weiß sie zu formulieren.

Auch innerhalb der ästhetischen Begründungen und der Diskurse der Künste generell im letzten Viertel des 20. Jahrhunderts können Meiers Position und sein Œuvre Folgerichtigkeit und Evidenz für sich beanspruchen. Gerade in diesem Zeitraum hat die Selbstreflexion der künstlerischen Gattungen auf ihre jeweils eigenen, historisch bereits durchgespielten Entwurfsvokabulare eklatant zugenommen. Die ästhetischen Programme der Reaktivierung reichen dabei von der Postmoderne bis zu den »Neuen Wilden« und dem »Neo-Geo« in der Malerei, über den »Neo-Barock« und diverse »Retro-Stile« im Produktdesign bis zum Dekonstruktivismus, der den russischen Konstruktivismus aufgreift. Dabei ist, verallgemeinernd gesagt, eine Verwandlung kreativer Prinzipien niemals bloß antiquarisch oder erschöpft sich im bloßen Zitat. Vielmehr geht es um eine schöpferische Adaption von Prinzipien historischer Entwürfe, deren Vokabular aber jeweils weiter gefaßt wird und sich sowohl produktionstechnisch wie ästhetisch mit Erkenntnissen und Empfindungen der Gegenwart verbündet. Wenn Thomas Mann im *Zauberberg* bemerkt: »Das Alte will das Neue sein und schminkt sich die Farbe des Lebens an«,[6] wenn andererseits Marcel Proust in seinem epochalen Werk *Jean Sauteuil* konstatiert, daß Phantasie »nicht auf die gegenwärtige Wirklichkeit und auch nicht auf die vergangene, vom Gedächtnis uns überlieferte Wirklichkeit (anwendbar sei), sondern vielmehr einzig jene vergangene Wirklichkeit, die in eine gegenwärtige Wirklichkeit eingefangen ist, umschwebe«,[7] und schließlich Friedrich Nietzsche in einem Essay festhält, daß es drei Arten gäbe, die Vergangenheit zu betrachten, die monumentalische, die antiquarische und die kritische,[8] dann sind damit Aspekte einer retrospektiven ästhetischen Rezeption beschrieben, aber keineswegs die Tiefe und die Bandbreite des kreativen Umgangs mit Traditionen erschöpfend charakterisiert.

ing artist, two-dimensionally in forming collages and three-dimensionally in forming sculptures. While Meier's buildings were extensively publicized and are generally known today among a wider public as well-known »landmarks« of building in our time, his other products, pictures, and sculptures are much less known and recognized.

The English architectural critic Charles Jencks has characterized Richard Meier as a »Late Modernist«. Independent from the fact that such »drawer« classifications over-generalize the factually rich variations of an individual artistic œuvre in a similar way like classical styles do with whole epochs, this term nevertheless describes some dominant convictions and design outlines of this artist. First of all, this description focuses on the slightly nostalgic disposition of the architect, who draws the strongest stimulus for his work from the first quarter of the 20th century. Furthermore, the prefix »late« stresses Meier's characteristic otherness from the everyday contemporary architectural »handwritings« of, for instance, Postmodernism, Minimalism, and Deconstructivism, views from which Meier keeps an overall critical distance. Finally, the term »Late Modern« stresses his concentration on the exclusive esthetic substrata of Modernism and Neue Sachlichkeit, particularly since the social and cultural context of today differ widely from those around 1900 or 1920. This contextual divergence can principally be compared with the ontology of museums, which for obvious reasons always detach their exhibits from their conditions of origin or use. In this respect, it is almost self-evident that Richard Meier for almost 30 years now belongs among the most successful masters of design of contemporary museums. Last, but not least, the term »Late Modern« evokes a Mannerist late phase of Modernism whose »classical time« is unretrievably by-gone. Oswald Spengler's biological philosophy of history which describes cultures as organisms which are principally subject to the cycles of bloom, ripeness, and decay, might have played a part here. Possibly, the epoque-shaping work on Mannerism published by Gustav René Hocke in 1957 was also a point of reference. Hocke describes Mannerism as a late style of the Renaissance.[4] The fact that Meier can be seen as a »mannerist of Modernism« with a certain justification has been continually stressed. This concerns refinements, sensibilities and a certain luxuriousness in the creative idiom, which were not contained in the »classical phase« of Modernism – and could not or did not want to be contained in it. This predisposition may simply result from the social distance which American architects from the East Coast of the USA might have from Europe. They referred to the European history of Modernism to a large degree through the filter of the »International Style«, propagated by Philip Johnson. But it may also result from Meier's temporary cooperation with the office of Bauhaus member Marcel Breuer who emigrated to New York. This figurative idea of »good old Europe«, which condenses and, at the same time, exculpates the social transformations of the Weimar Republic and its forceful end in National Socialism as well as its socio-utopian origin and expections in favor of a pacified, rather dominant esthetic experience. This background has also shaped Meier's understanding of European traditions. In order not to be misunderstood, this is the description of a philosophical stance and not its criticism, since the artistic results of this philosophy are brilliant in a double sense of the word, intellectually and esthetically. But maybe, an understanding which is decidedly cultural-political can most adequately explain the stylistical term »Late Modern«. Because Meier's architectural language which generally orients itself along the idea of »white Modernism« has returned something to Europe and especially to Germany which had been isolated, ostracized, expelled, and persecuted by the National Socialists. With reference to the Museum für Angewandte Kunst in Frankfurt, his first building realized in Europe, Meier remembers still today: »When the building opened, I said how important it was for me to do the building as an American, an architect, and a Jew, because I had helped to build a link between what was destroyed in World War II and the present.«[5] Indeed, Meier has given back something to Germany, to Europe – changed, updated, and newly interpreted –, something which had been buried, finished, driven out, and wiped out. In this sense, next to Meier's esthetic brilliance stands his highly political nature. On such a level, Meier's »Late Modernism« is political indeed. It intervenes in the artistic situation of modern-day Europe. It takes its own position, and it knows how to formulate it.

Even within the esthetic justifications and discourses among the arts in general during the last quarter of the 20th century, Meier's position and his œuvre stand for logical sequence and evidence. Especially during that time span the self-reflection among the artistic genres about their peculiar vocabulary of design grew strikingly. The esthetic programs of reactivation extend from Postmodernism to the »Neue Wilde« and the »Neo-Geo« in painting, from »Neo-Baroque« and diverse other »retro-styles« in the field of product design up to Deconstructivism which refers to Russian Constructivism. Generally speaking, an alteration of creative principles is here never merely antiquarian, nor does it exhaust itself with simple quotes. It is rather concerned with a creative adaptation of principles taken from historical precepts whose vocabulary is in each case more generally defined and which associates itself with the insights and sentiments of our time. Thomas Mann, for instance, remarks in *The Magic Mountain* that »The old wants to be the new and uses the make-up color of life«.[6] Marcel Proust, on the other hand states in his epoque-shaping work *Jean Santeuil* that fantasy should not be applied »to the reality of the present, nor that of the past, which our memory has transmitted to us, but rather that it solely hovers around that past reality which has entered into a reality of the present.«[7] Finally, Friedrich Nietzsche confirms in one of his essays that there are three possible ways to look at the past, namely the monumental, the antiquarian, and the critical.[8] Whithin these statements all aspects of a retrospective esthetic reception are described, while this neither completely characterizes either depth or breadth of creative dealing with traditions.

Objekte für Räume

1984 erschien die erste Möbelkollektion von Richard Meier, produziert von jenem Unternehmen Knoll International, das durch die Entwürfe des deutschen Emigranten Mies van der Rohe und später durch die Übernahme des italienischen Unternehmens Gavina mit den Entwürfen von Marcel Breuer ebenso bekannt wurde wie durch die 50er-Jahre-Entwürfe von Eliel und Eero Saarinen, Harry Bertoia, Isamu Noguchi und ab den 60er Jahren durch die Office-Möbel von Florence Knoll, der Mitinhaberin und Ehefrau des früh verstorbenen Firmengründers Hans Knoll. Meiers Kollektion besteht aus sechs Ahorn-Holzmöbeln mit unterschiedlichem schwarzen Finish. Aus grazilen Vierkantstäben hat er eine Liege, zwei unterschiedlich hohe Tische mit Abrundungen der quadratischen Tischplatten in großen Radien, einen Stuhl, einen Barhocker sowie einen kleinen Beistellhocker konstruiert. Die Kollektion bezieht sich formal auf den Wiener Jugendstil und hier vor allem auf Josef Hoffmann, der nicht ohne Grund den Spitznahmen »Quadratl-Hoffmann« hatte, sowie Otto Wagner. Auch Meiers Möbel sind geometrische Exerzitien im Raum, rasterverliebt und selbst da noch rektangulär, wo es um ergonomische Anpassung an Körperformen geht. Der organische Schalen- und Halbschalenstil von Charles Eames oder Alvar Aalto ist seine Sache nicht. So ist Meiers Stuhl ein geometrisches Raumgitter, lediglich tischhoch und im Lehnenbereich aus drei exakten Halbkreisen aufgebaut, die sich mit gleichem Radius in der geschlossenen Sitzfläche fortsetzen. Völlig schmuck- und ornamentlos, erinnert der Stuhl trotzdem an Josef Hoffmanns »Fledermaussessel« (1905) sowie vor allem an Otto Wagners »Postsparkassenstuhl« (1905). Hat der erste eine identische Anmutung in seiner Struktur, auch wenn er durch kleine Kugeln an den Gelenkstellen zwischen waagerechter Lehne und senkrechten Stäben geschmückt ist, so der zweite eine noch stärkere Affinität in seinen Dimensionen und Proportionen. Auch erinnert Meiers Knoll-Stuhl von ferne an jenen von Walter Gropius, den dieser 1911 für die Alfelder Faguswerke gestaltet hat. Die senkrechte Halbzylinderform des Stuhls hat ebenfalls bereits Josef Hoffmann 1906 in einer »Salon-Garnitur« angewendet, wenn auch mit dreimal, jeweils zu viert rhythmisierten senkrechten Rundstäben. Demgegenüber wirkt Meiers schwarzer Stuhl minimalistischer, mehr wie ein Raumgitter, bei dem die Verbindungen von senkrechten und waagerechten Vierkantstäben nahtlos-exakt übereinandergreifen. Die frühe Naturholzvariante des Meierschen Knoll-Stuhls aus Rundstäben zeigt den Ursprung des Entwurfs, der sich auf Zeiten vor der Stahlrohr-Freischwingerära der 1920er Jahre bezieht. Meier überblendet also Charakteristika von Hoffmann-, Wagner- und Gropius-Entwürfen und reduziert dann dieses komplexe Stuhlbild auf Gemeinsamkeiten in ihrer Struktur. Damit erzeugt er eine historisch aufgeladene, gleichwohl zeitgenössische Eleganz, die auf vergleichbare Weise auch die Tische und Hocker seiner Kollektion charakterisiert. Die Liege dagegen, sowohl in der Form der Lederauflagefläche wie in der Gesamtproportion jener berühmten »Chaise longue« Le Corbusiers von 1929 verwandt, die dieser für den Pariser Pavillon »Esprit nouveau« entworfen hatte und die heute als Liege LC4 von der Mailänder Firma Cassina wieder produziert wird,[9] hat als Basis ein geometrisches schwarzes Quadrat-Raumgitter aus Vierkantprofilen, welches sich geradezu störrisch rektangulär der körperfreundlich geschwungenen Liegefläche entgegenstellt. Diese Liegefläche erinnert im übrigen mit ihrer Quersteppung auch an die von Charles Eames entworfene sogenannte »Billy-Wilder-Liege« (1968), produziert von Herman Miller und Vitra sowie an Mies van der Rohes MR-Liege (1927 bis 1929) von Knoll International. Das Raumgitter endet zum Boden hin in zwei Oval-Segmentkurven, die leichtes Schaukeln erlauben und damit ein altes Thonet-Prinzip variieren. Die serielle Rigidität des Stabgitters übersteigt bei weitem seine statische Funktion und Notwendigkeit. So ist ein durchaus manierierter Lounge-Chair entstanden, bei dem das Durchdeklinieren des die gesamte Kollektion charakterisierenden Entwurfsvokabulars fast zum Selbstzweck geworden ist. Gerade hier bei der Liege mit dem Raumgitter und der ergonomisch sensiblen Liegefläche stehen zwei Formprinzipien in scharfem Kontrast gegeneinander mit dem Ergebnis formaler Zwiespältigkeit. Nicht Harmonie, sondern Spannung, nicht konstruktive Einheitlichkeit im Sinne der klassischen Moderne, sondern hybride Vieldeutigkeit im Sinne postmoderner Überlagerungen: fürwahr ein »spätmodernes« Produkt. Vielleicht aber hat Richard Meier mit dieser Liege auch eine leicht selbstironische Überzeichnung seines Vokabulars im Sinn gehabt. Man geht wohl kaum fehl, in dem fast demonstrativ überzogenen Basisgerüst der Liege auch einen augenzwinkernden Kommentar zu Le Corbusier, Mies oder Alvar Aalto zu sehen. Auch wird damit die räumliche Konzeption der Möbel des holländischen De Stijl à la Rietveld durch Übertreibung ihrer Prinzipien endgültig zur Historie erklärt, vielleicht auch verklärt. Um Susan Sontag zu paraphrasieren: Man kann jede Kanonisierung durch die Übertreibung ihrer inhärenten Strukturen wirkungsvoll in Frage stellen. Und wem würden gerade bei den großen Tischen mit ihren über Kreuz gestellten parallelen Auflagerstrukturen nicht die Möbel des Schotten Charles Rennie Mackintosh in den Sinn kommen?

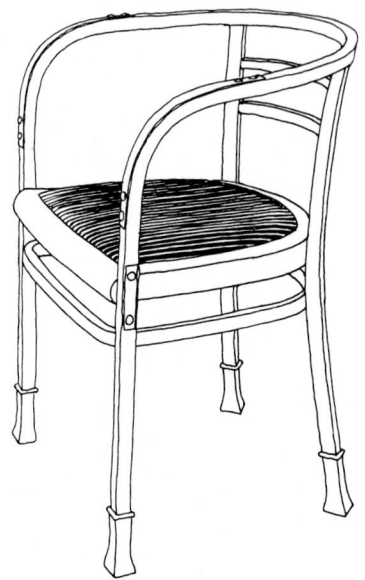

Knoll International jedenfalls hatte mit diesem Programm, welches, wie deutlich wurde, bewußt »europäische« Züge zeigt, einmal mehr seine Kompetenz dokumentiert, bedeutendes Mobiliar von Architekten zu initiieren und zu produzieren. Ähnlich wie bei Mackintosh sind diese Möbel in die ornamentale Kraft der reinen Geometrie verliebt und setzen sie auch durch; gegen die angeblich zwingenden Gesetze des Komforts setzen sie Struktur und visuelle Ordnung. Schönheit entsteht für Meier hier durch die dreidimensionalen Variationen einer geometrischen Matrix, denen sich die Produkte anschmiegsam anzupassen haben. Und wahrscheinlich ist es dieses Beharren auf der Ordnung und dem System, ja dem Diskurs der dreidimensionalen Gitter – die auch an den minimalistischen amerikanischen Bildhauer Donald Judd denken lassen –, welches dieser Kollektion ihren unverwechselbaren Charme und Charakter verleiht.

Etwa zehn Jahre später hat Richard Meier eine weitere vierteilige Möbelkollektion für die

1. Otto Wagner, Stuhl für die Postsparkasse in Wien, 1905.
2. Josef Hoffmann, »Fledermaus-Sessel«, ca. 1907.
3. Le Corbusier, Chaise lounge LC4, 1928; Thonet, heute Cassina.
4. Ludwig Mies van der Rohe, Liege der MR-Kollektion, 1927–29; Bamberg Metallwerkstätten, heute Knoll International.
5. Charles und Ray Eames, Eames Chaise (»Billy-Wilder-Liege«), 1968; Herman Miller und Vitra.

1. Otto Wagner, chair for the Post Office Savings Bank, Vienna, 1905.
2. Josef Hoffmann, »Fledermaus Chair«, c. 1907.
3. Le Corbusier, LC4 chaise lounge, 1928; Thonet, today Cassina.
4. Ludwig Mies van der Rohe, lounge chair of the MR Collection, 1927–29; Bamberg Metallwerkstätten; today Knoll International.
5. Charles and Ray Eames, Eames Chaise (»Lounge Chair for Billy Wilder«), 1968; Herman Miller and Vitra.

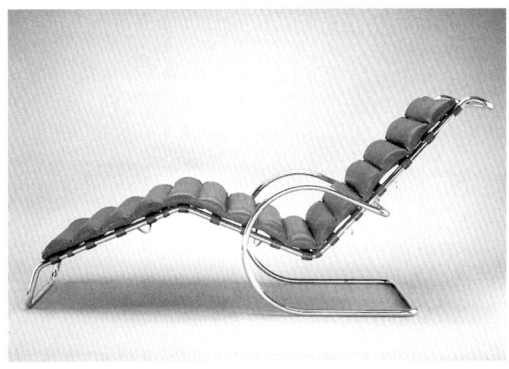

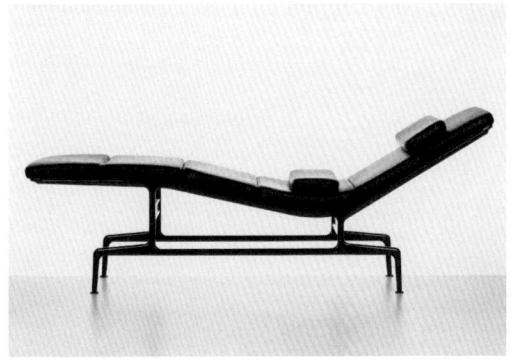

Objects for rooms

In 1984, Richard Meier's first furniture collection was offered to the public. It was produced by the same firm of Knoll International which had become well known through designs by the German emigré Mies van der Rohe and later by its annexation of the Italian firm of Gavina with the designs by Marcel Breuer as well as through the designs of the 50s by Eliel and Eero Saarinen, Harry Bertoia, and Isamu Noguchi, and, starting in the 60's, by the designs for office furniture by Florence Knoll, the co-owner and wife of the early-deceased founder of the firm, Hans Knoll. Meier's collection consists of six maple-wood pieces of varying black finish. With delicate rectangular posts he fashioned a lounge, two tables with round-edged tops of large circumference which are of different height, a chair, a bar stool, and a small side table. The collection formally refers back to the Art Nouveau of Vienna and here especially to Josef Hoffmann, whose nickname was not without reason »Quadratl-Hoffmann«, and to Otto Wagner. Meier's furniture pieces are also geometrical exercises in space. They appear fond of screen patterns, and even then still rectangular when an ergonomic adaptation to human body was involved. The organic bowl and half-bowl shapes of Charles Eames or Alvar Aalto do not attract him. Thus, Meier's chair represents a geometric space grid. It is only of table hight and constructed of three exact semi-circles in the area of the arm rests which continue with equal diameter towards the tightly constructed seat. The chair which is without decoration or ornament, nevertheless reminds of the »Fledermaus Chair« (1907) by Josef Hoffmann and especially of Otto Wagner's chair for the Post Office Savings Bank (1905). While the first posseses an identical grace of structure, even if it is decorated with small spheres at its axes between the horizontal arm rests and the vertical posts, the second shows an even stronger affinity in its dimensions and proportions. Also, Meier's Knoll chair distantly resembles the one by Walter Gropius created in 1911 for the Fagus factory in Alfeld. The vertical, half-cylindrical shape of the chair has been applied already by Josef Hoffmann in 1906 in his »Salon Set«, even if there three times four vertical, round posts followed each other rhythmically. In comparison, Meier's black chair appears more Minimalistic, rather like a space grid, in which the connections between its vertical and horizontal posts seamlessly converge. The early variant of natural wood of Meier's Knoll chair with its round posts shows the origin of its design. It reminds of the time prior to the era of the cantilevered »steel pipe« construction during the 1920's. Meier, thus, combines the characteristics of Hoffmann, Wagner, and Gropius designs and reduces the image of his chair to the commonalities of their mutual design structures. In this way, he produces an image of contemporary elegance, resplendent with history. All of these attributes equally characterize the tables and stools of his collection. The lounge, on the other hand, refers in its form, with its leather-covered surface, and in its total proportions to that famous »Chaise Longue« of Le Corbusier from 1929. It was designed for the Paris Pavilion »Esprit nouveau« and is reproduced today as lounge »LC4« by the firm of Cassina in Milan.[9] Its base consists of black, geometrical space grid of squares showing four-corner profiles. But these contrast almost determinedly and rectangularly with curved surface lines of the lounge seat which easily adapts to the outlines of the human body. Besides, this seat surface with its cross-quilting also brings to mind the image of Charles Eames's »Lounge Chair for Billy Wilder« (1968), which is produced by Herman Miller and Vitra. It also reminds of Mies van der Rohe's MR lounge chair (1927–29) produced today by Knoll International. The space grid ends towards the floor in two oval curve segments, which permit easy rocking and which therefore represent a variation of an older Thonet principle. The serial rigidity of the grid by far out-functions the necessity for a static equilibrium. In this manner, a totally mannerist lounge chair has been created. Altogether, the full declension of the design vocabulary which characterizes the entire collection has almost become a necessity in itself. Especially here, with the lounge with its space grid and its ergonomically sensitive seat surface two principles of form sharply contrast each other resulting in a formal duplicity. Not harmony, but tension, not constructive uniformity in the Modernist sense, but a hybrid ambiguity in the sense of Postmodern cross-layering exists: a truly »Late-Modern« product. But maybe, Richard Meier had some slight self-ironical touch-up of his vocabulary in mind when he created this lounge. One can hardly err when one envisages a tiny wink of commentary with Le Corbusier, Mies, or Aalto in the almost demonstratively exaggerated basic structure of the lounge. In this context, the spatial conception of the furnishings by the Dutch De Stijl movement in the manner of Rietveld, finally becomes outdated or maybe just transfigured, because of the exaggeration of their principles. In order to paraphrase Susan Sontag, one can make each canonization successfully questionable through an exaggeration of its inherent structures. And who, in looking particularly at the large tables with their parallel layer structures put crosswise, would not be reminded of the furniture of the Scotsman Charles Rennie Mckintosh?

By offering this program, which consciously shows »European« features, Knoll International had definitely and once again documented its competency in initiating and producing remarkable furniture pieces created by architects. Similarly to that of Mackintosh, this furniture has a particular charm in the ornamental power of its plain geometry, and it makes a convincing point, even against the alleged compelling laws of comfort, presenting structure and visual order. For Meier, beauty is created here through the three-dimensional variations of a geometrical matrix to which idea the material objects have to adapt smoothly. It is most likely that his insistence on order and the geometrical system, even the structural discourse within the three-dimensional lattice work – also reminding of the Minimalist American sculptor Donald Judd – lends the distinctive charm and character to this collection.

About ten years later, Richard Meier designed a second four-piece furniture collection for the American firm of Stow Davis. It consists of a couch, a chair, a bench, and a reception desk.

amerikanische Firma Stow Davis entworfen. Sie besteht aus einem Sofa, einem Kurzsofa, einer Sitzbank und einem Rezeptionsmöbel. Die drei Sitzmöbel sind optisch betont flache, breit gelagerte Raumebenen, jeweils bestehend aus weiß lackierten Holzplatten, die auf drei unterschiedlich dimensionierten schwarzen Holzscheiben auflagern, welche zudem in Breite und Tiefe asymmetrisch angeordnet sind. Schon damit wird auf die »freie« Raumscheibenästhetik der holländischen De-Stijl-Möbel à la Rietveld Bezug genommen, etwa auf seinen berühmten Stuhl »Berlin« von 1923 sowie eine vergleichbare Bank von 1928. Verstärkt wird dieser Bezug nochmals sowohl bei dem Sofa als auch dem Kurzsofa, die beide weit auskragende asymmetrische Ablageflächen nach einer bzw. beiden Schmalseiten hin ausfahren. Aber auch Meiers Affinität zu Marcel Breuer, in dessen Architekturbüro seine eigene Karriere prägende erste Impulse erfuhr, wird hier deutlich. Breuer, der über das Bauhaus mit Rietveld Kontakt hatte, war ebenfalls asymmetrischen Raumvolumen in Form horizontal und vertikal auskragender Scheiben bei manchen seiner frühen, noch in Europa entstandenen Möbel nicht abhold. Bei Meiers Sitzmöbeln sind Sofa und Kurzsofa mit volumigen, durch quadratische Steppungen unterbrochenen schwarzen Lederpolstern und schwarzen Lederrollen als Rückenstützen bestückt. So stellt sich auch die Anmutung englischer Klubmöbel ein, allerdings gefiltert durch eine Prise Eileen Grayscher metropolenmondäner Eleganz und Asymmetrie. Andererseits schwingt auch ein bißchen der Präriestil von Frank Lloyd Wright mit, so daß es schlußendlich dann doch sehr amerikanische Möbel sind. Die standhohe Rezeption eignet sich für Hotels und Agenturen, aber auch für Architekturbüros, ist ebenfalls in Schwarz und Weiß gehalten und ebenso asymmetrisch aus waagrechten und senkrechten Holzscheiben frei komponiert. Erneut also ist diese Stow-Davis-Kollektion durch mannigfaltige Bezüge auf die europäische Moderne charakterisiert. Hier aber, mehr als bei der ersten Möbelkollektion, handelt es sich um allansichtige, pragmatische Raumskulpturen, deren additiver formaler Eigensinn ihnen Manifestcharakter verleiht. Gerade diese Serie verweist aber auch auf die »Durchdringungsästhetik« von Volumen und Flächen der Architekturen von Richard Meier, ja sie paraphrasiert sie geradezu.

Die sich bereits hier ankündigende mondäne Charakteristik kennzeichnet noch deutlicher einen Flügel, den Meier 1995–97 für den deutschen Klavierbauer Ibach entworfen hat. Dieses Musikinstrument hat einen schwarzen, hochglanzlackierten Korpus, betont seine Raumkanten und wirkt dadurch besonders architektonisch-statuarisch. Auch die Pedale des Flügels und der dazu gehörige Klavierhocker sind architektonisch aufgefaßt. Andererseits wirkt das Pianovolumen schwebend, weil es auf flachen, verchromten, zudem asymmetrisch positionierten Füßen steht. Besonders bei geöffnetem Deckel, der durch eine versenkbare »Sinuskurve« arretiert wird, erschließt sich die räumliche Komplexität dieses Instrumentes. Insgesamt ist dieses »Grand piano« Luxus pur und wurde nur zweimal gebaut. Es ist ein öffentliches Schaustück, für Konzerte eines Liberace oder Elton John geeignet, mehr dem Showbiz als dem Konservatorium zugehörig.

Neben Mobiliar hat Meier für das amerikanische Unternehmen Baldinger auch Leuchten entworfen: zwei Wandlampen, jeweils rektangular, deren Licht mittels opalisierender Acrylgläser weich gestreut wird. Die vor der Wand situierten, flach gebogenen Scheiben sind weniger Gehäuse einer Lichtquelle als deren Einbindung in architektonisch begriffene Abwicklungen. Auch die Halterungen der Acrylglasscheiben mit polierten Chromoberflächen sind eher Elemente eines produktkulturellen »Architekturdiskurses« als Ausdruck eines technoid optimierten Industriedesigns.

Das Griffeprogramm für Fenster und Türen von Meier, produziert von Valli & Valli, ist eine gleichfalls mikroarchitektonisch aufgefaßte Palette. Heute sind die internen, nicht sichtbaren Teile eines Griffprogramms technisch und sicherheitstechnisch so optimiert, daß man, jedenfalls in dieser Hinsicht, mit Fug und Recht von Standardisierung sprechen kann. Was gestalterisch zu tun bleibt, beschränkt sich auf die Griffe selbst, auf ihre Haptik und stilistische Anmutung. Dabei ist die Gestaltungsaufgabe, Räume auf- und abzuschließen, spätestens seit Wittgenstein mit philosophischem Anspruch unterlegt. Griffe, Greifen und »Begreifen« bilden eine mentale Einheit. Der deutsche Designer Otl Aicher hat dies so ausgedrückt:

»geist ist offenbar weniger in der transzendenz als in der hand angesiedelt. weil die hand greifen kann, kann auch das denken begreifen. weil die hand fassen kann, erfassen wir auch etwas in unserem kopf. weil die hand etwas vor uns hinstellen kann, können wir auch etwas durch denken darstellen. weil die hand legen kann, legen wir auch im denken etwas dar. und wir legen nicht nur dar, wir überlegen, wir legen aufeinander, übereinander. wir stellen nicht nur fest, wir stellen auch auf, eine neue these zum beispiel. wir begreifen nicht nur, wir erfassen nicht nur, wir befassen uns auch mit etwas, wir wenden und drehen etwas und gelangen schließlich zu einer auffassung.

etwas begriffen haben, steht nicht nur in einer einen bildlichen analogie mit dem tatsächlichen greifen. die kultur des denkens setzt eine kultur der hand als einem subtilen, sensitiven organ voraus. ... der begriff ist das begriffene.«[10]

Meiers hochglanzverchromte Tür- und Fenstergriffe, ergänzt durch Knäufe, Rundrosetten und Zimmerschlüssel, zelebrieren wie manche seiner Kerzenleuchter und Bilderhalter einen additiven Formaufbau, der ergonomische Greifqualitäten vernachlässigt. Auch hier wieder interessiert den Entwerfer in erster Linie die Ausponderierung und gegenseitige Durchdringung geometrischer Körper wie Quader, Würfel, Prisma und Zylinder.

6. Thomas Rietveld, Stuhl »Berlin«, 1923; Cassina.
7. Marcel Breuer, Schreibtisch mit Bücherregal, 1924.

6. Thomas Rietveld, »Berlin« chair, 1923; Cassina.
7. Marcel Breuer, desk with book shelf, 1924.

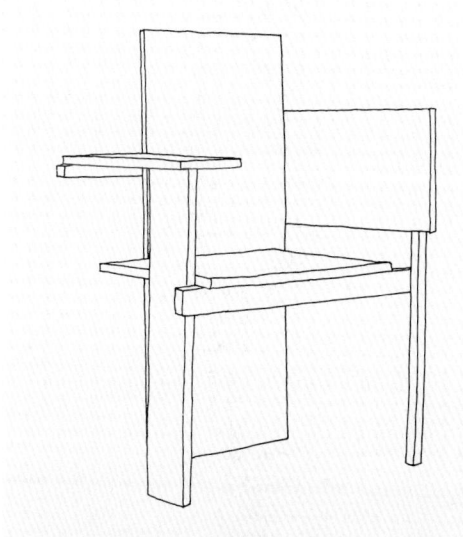

The three pieces of furniture for seating stress optically flat, widely layed-out spatial planes, each of them consisting of wood panels lackered in white. These panels rest on black wooden disks of varying dimensions and asymmetrical arrangement. This way already, a connection is established to the »free« spatial disks of the Dutch De Stijl furniture in the manner of Rietveld. One may, for instance, remember the example of the famous »Berlin« chair of 1923 and the example of a comparable bank of 1928. The connection is further strengthened with regard to the couch and the chair. Both exhibit far-extending asymmetrical side-table extensions, either to one of the narrow sides or to both. But there appears to be another affinity of Meier's, namely to the concepts and designs of Marcel Breuer in whose architectural bureau Meier's own career received its first determing influences. Breuer stood in contact with Rietveld when he was in the Bauhaus, and he also used asymmetrical spatial structures in the form of horizontally and vertically extended disks in some of his early furnishings which still were created on European soil. With Meier's furniture pieces for seating, couch and chair have voluminous black leather cushions embellished with quilting in quadratic designs and black rolls as backrests. This creates an atmoshphere of the grace of English club furniture, but filtered through a breeze of the fashionable metropolitan elegance and asymmetry in the manner of Eileen Gray. On the other hand, a whiff of Frank Lloyd Wright's prairie style may also be felt, so that in their final representation, these pieces are quite American by nature, after all. The high reception desk is suitable for hotels and business agencies, but also for architectural offices. It is equally kept in black and white and is also composed asymmetrically of horizontal and vertical disks which are loosely arranged. Once again, this Stow Davis collection exemplifies a variety of connections with the European Modern Movement. But these, more than the first furniture collection, are pragmatic space sculptures facing in all directions, whose additive formal insistence gives them the aspect of a manifesto. Especially this series points towards the »esthetic of fusion« with volumes and planes of Richard Meier's architectural designs, in fact it paraphrases them.

The fashionable character which is here indicated, further defines itself with a grand piano which Meier designed 1995–97 for the German piano builder Ibach. This musical instrument has a black, highly varnished body, stresses its spacious corners and thus creates a special, statuary architectural effect. The pedals and the piano seat reveal an architectural concept as well. On the other hand, the entire volume of the instrument seems to float, since it rests on flat, asymmetrically positioned chrome bases. Especially with the instrument lid open and arrested by a submersible »sinus curve«, the spatial complexity of this instrument becomes apparent. Overall, this design represents pure »grand piano« luxury and exists only in two copies. It is a public showpiece, suitable for concerts by Liberace or Elton John and rather belonging to showbiz than to a conservatory.

Besides furniture, Meier has also designed lighting fixtures for the American firm of Baldinger: two wall sconces, each time rectangular, whose light spreads diffusely by way of opalising acrylic glasses. The panes have shallow curves and extend away from the wall, less representing covers for the source of light than attachments in an architecturally perceived process. The soccets of the acrylic panes with their polished chrome-plated surfaces are equally rather elements of a product-oriented »discourse in architecture« than an expression of an optimized technoid industrial design.

Meier's collection of handles for windows and doors, produced by Valli & Valli, also represents a micro-architectural palette. In our day, the internal and invisible parts of such a collection of handles have been improved so much, in a technical and safety-technical sense, that, in this respect, one can rightfully speak of standardization. What remains to be done from the side of design is restricted to the grips themselves and pertains to their haptics and their stylistic grace. The task for their spatial arrangement and application and that of how they open and close individual rooms, has been undergirded philosophically, at the latest, by the ideas of Wittgenstein. Handles or grips and »gripping« represent a mental unity. The German designer Otl Aicher has expressed this idea as follows:

»Mind is apparently seated less in transcendence than in the hand. Because the hand can grasp, thought can also grasp. Because our hand can take hold of something our heads can take hold of it as well. Because the hand can present, thinking can represent. Because the hand can lay things down, thinking can lay things down as well. And we do not just lay things down, we overlay, lay things on top of each other. We do not just set things firmly in mind, we set things up, a new theory for example, we do not just grasp, do not just take hold, we take a view of things, twist them and turn them finally arriving at a point of view.

Having grasped something mentally is not just a pictorial analogy with physical grasping. The culture of thinking requires a culture of the hand as a subtle, sensitive organ. ... The concept is what is conceived.«[10]

Meier's door and window handles with their shining chrome-plating, together with pulls, round rosettes and door keys, celebrate, like some of his candelabra and picture stands, an additive formal structure which neglects the ergonomic qualities of grasping. Here as well, the designer is primarily interested in balancing out and interlocking geometrical shapes such as rectangular blocks, cubes, prisms, and cylinders.

1. Stuhl, 1982; Knoll International, New York.
2. Stuhl, 1978; Knoll International, New York.
3, 4. Liege, 1982; Knoll International, New York.

1. Chair, 1982; Knoll International, New York.
2. Chair, 1978; Knoll International, New York.
3, 4. Lounge chair, 1982; Knoll International, New York.

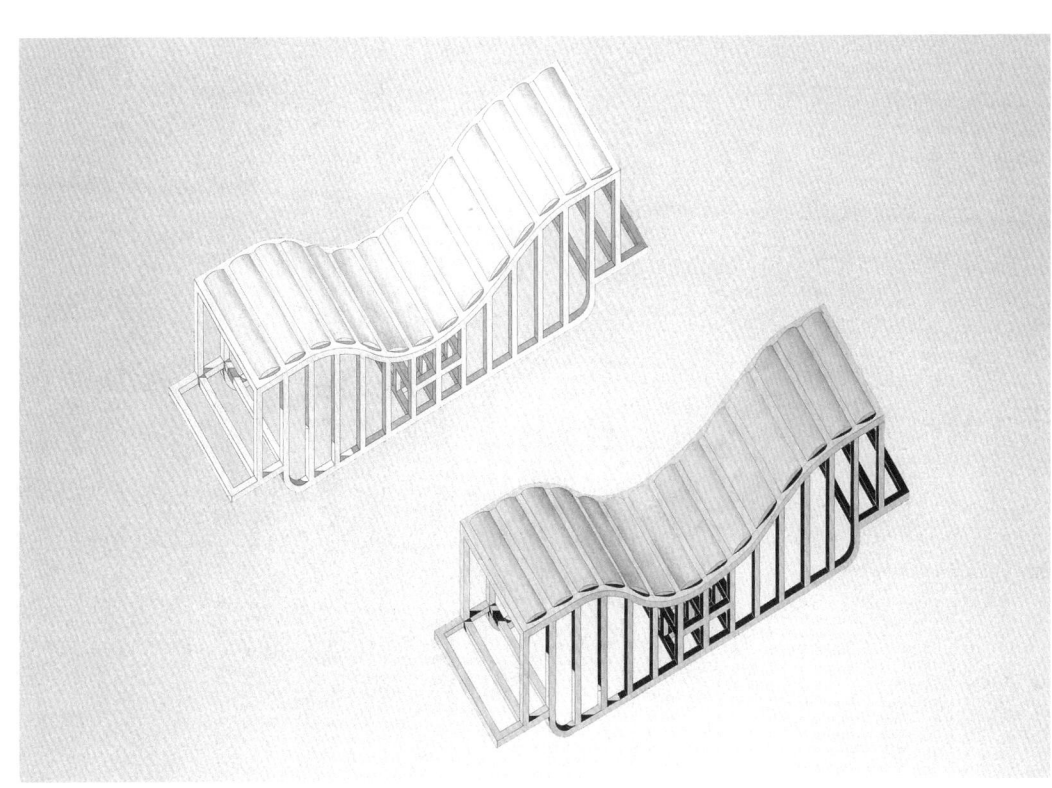

5. Eßtisch, 1982; Knoll International, New York.
6. Couchtisch, 1982; Knoll International, New York.
7. Konzertflügel, 1995; Rud. Ibach Sohn, Schwelm, Deutschland.

5. High table, 1982; Knoll International, New York.
6. Low table, 1982; Knoll International, New York.
7. Grand piano, 1995; Rud. Ibach Sohn, Schwelm, Germany.

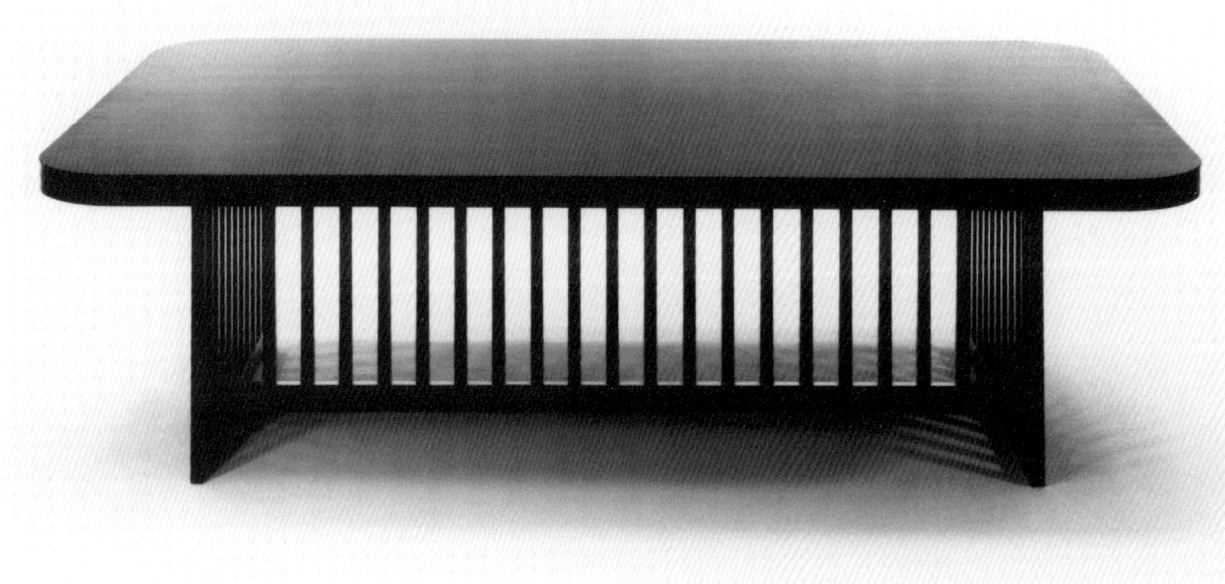

8. Kurzsofa, 1992; Stow Davis, Grand Rapids, USA.
9. Sofa, 1992; Stow Davis, Grand Rapids, USA.

8. Chair, 1992; Stow Davis, Grand Rapids, USA.
9. Sofa, 1992; Stow Davis, Grand Rapids, USA.

10. Sitzbank, 1992; Stow Davis, Grand Rapids, USA.
11. Empfangstresen, 1992; Stow Davis, Grand Rapids, USA.

10. Bench, 1992; Stow Davis, Grand Rapids, USA.
11. Reception desk, 1992; Stow Davis, Grand Rapids, USA.

12. Wandleuchte »Max«, 1989; Louis Baldinger & Sons, Inc., New York.
13. Wand- oder Deckenleuchte »Ana«, 1989; Louis Baldinger & Sons, Inc., New York.

12. »Max« wall light, 1989; Louis Baldinger & Sons, Inc., New York.
13. »Ana« wall or ceiling light, 1989; Louis Baldinger & Sons, Inc., New York.

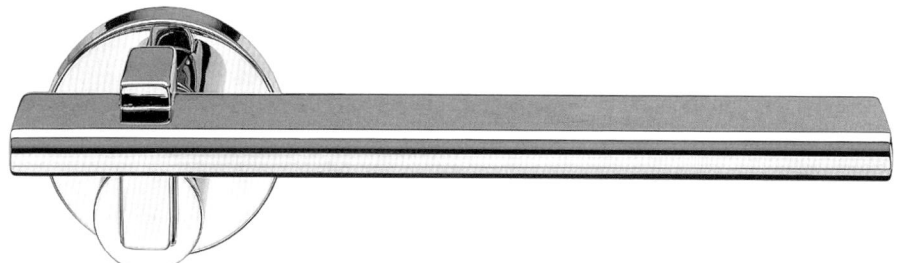

14–20. Serie »RM Novantotto«, 1994; Fusital (Valli & Valli), New York.
14. Türdrücker.
15. Fenstergriff.
16. Fenstergriff.
17. Türschließer.
18. Türgriff.
19. Knopfdrücker.
20. Rosetten und Türschlüssel.

14–20. »RM Novantotto« series, 1994; Fusital (Valli & Valli), New York.
14. Doorhandle.
15. Window pull.
16. Window pull.
17. Privacy lock set.
18. Pull handle.
19. Doorknob.
20. Key-hole plate and doorkey.

Objekte für Tisch und Schreibtisch

Es hat eine ganz eigene Folgerichtigkeit, wenn Richard Meier, eingedenk seiner Vorbilder der Wiener Schule wie Loos, Hoffmann oder Wagner, auch Glas-, Porzellan- und Silberprodukte für den gedeckten Tisch entwirft. Während die Wiener Jugendstil-Geometristen aber auf das traditionsreiche Böhmer Glashandwerk zurückgreifen konnten, werden Meiers Tisch- und Schreibtischprodukte in den USA produziert. Dabei haben er und viele andere nicht nur amerikanische Architekten und Designer in dem New Yorker Unternehmen Swid Powell ein ehrgeiziges Produzentenpaar gefunden, das in den 1980er Jahren mit Autoren-Design Furore machte, welches ebenso die Entwerferpersönlichkeiten und –psychologien in den Vordergrund stellte wie Alessi oder Vitra in Europa. Allenfalls Knoll International hatte in den USA in den Jahrzehnten nach dem Krieg eine ähnliche Strategie verfolgt; ein Unternehmen allerdings, welches, wie gesagt, ursprünglich europäisch geprägt war. Im Bereich der Glas-, Silber- und Porzellanwaren fehlte eine solche Firma in den USA lange und war auch nicht durch limitierte Galerieprodukte zu ersetzen, die es immer einmal wieder gab. Als daher 1980 Nan Swid und Addie Powell, von denen die erstere Designberaterin für Produktentwicklung bei Knoll International und die zweite Vizepräsidentin der Verkaufsabteilung in ebendiesem Unternehmen war, ihre Firma gründeten, konnten sie auf eine Entwerferriege zurückgreifen, die damals fast vollständig das zeitgenössische »Who is who« der renommierten, und das hieß damals postmodern beeinflußten, Gestalter versammelte: Robert Venturi, Robert A. M. Stern, Richard Meier, Stanley Tigerman und Margaret McCurry, Charles Gwathmey und Robert Siegel, Michael Graves, Steven Holl und Arquitectonica aus den USA, Ettore Sottsass, George Sowden, Hans Hollein, Trix und Robert Haussmann aus Europa, Arata Isozaki aus Japan. Eine solche Phalanx international renommierter, dabei jeweils höchst individueller Entwurfsstrategien war bis dahin in den USA überhaupt seit den Zeiten Frank Lloyd Wrights und Louis Sullivans bei den in Rede stehenden Produktgattungen nicht mehr realisiert worden.[11] Meier bemerkte zu dieser Initiative: »Ich mag Nans und Addies Enthusiasmus, ihre unkomplizierte, fast naive Art, Dinge anzugehen und zu prüfen, wie man sie realisieren kann. Ohne ihre Ausdauer und Hingabe, Dinge zu realisieren, würde diese Initiative auseinanderfallen.«[12]

Und Paul Goldberger schätzt diese Initiative wohl richtig ein, wenn er konstatiert: »Für die Architektur war dies eine Gelegenheit, die Verbindung zwischen Architektur und angewandten Künsten erneut zu etablieren. Historisch gesprochen, waren Architekten früher für sehr viel mehr als nur ihre Gebäude verantwortlich, aber seit der Zeit der Wiener Werkstätten, die Josef Hoffmann 1903 gründete, hat es ein solches Studio wie Swid Powell nicht mehr gegeben.«[13] Diese Aussage gilt allerdings nur für die USA, denn in Europa hat seit nunmehr einem dreiviertel Jahrhundert die italienische Firma Alessi genau dies getan. Im Grunde war und ist Swid Powell die amerikanische Antwort auf Alessi.

Schaut man sich die Silber- und Glasprodukte Richard Meiers für Swid Powell an, dann wird zumindest dem europäisch geschulten Auge ein »Déjà-vu« besonderer Art beschert, denn sie wirken überwiegend geradezu wie eine Reinkarnation des geometrischen Wiener Jugendstils: und das mitten in Manhattan. Meier hat über 40 Produkte aus Silber für Swid Powell realisiert: Etwa zehn Silberschalen und Tabletts, einen Serviettenhalter und eine Karaffe mit Silberaufsatz sowie eine Mini-Amphore für den gedeckten Tisch, aber auch Bestecke und Vorlegebestecke. Dazu kommen die Accessoires für den Schreibtisch oder das Sideboard, Photographie-Rahmen, Brieföffner und Stiftbehälter, Briefständer und Leselupe, Heftklammerboxen, aber auch Lesezeichen, Geldscheinhalter und ein Schlüsselring. Damit ergibt sich eine fast vollständige Produktpalette jener Gegenstände, die man im privaten oder beruflichen Bereich unmittelbar als »Personal Design« um sich herum hat. Später kamen dann noch vier silberne Tauftassen für Kleinkinder sowie ein Menorah-Leuchter aus poliertem Aluminium hinzu. Die Verbindung zwischen seiner Architektur und den Entwürfen für Swid Powell ebenso wie seine Motivation für diese Entwüfe beschreibt Meier präzise: »Ich beziehe diese Produkte deshalb auf meine Architektur, weil sie eine direkte Beziehung zu mir selbst haben. Was ich entwerfe, sind nicht einfach Dinge, mit denen ich leben möchte, sondern Dinge, die ich brauche. So brauche ich Photorahmen für die Photos meiner Kinder, und ich brauche Schalen für Nüsse und Konfekt. Ich entwerfe nicht zuletzt deshalb für Swid Powell, weil ich auf dem Markt und den Geschäften keine Produkte gefunden habe, mit denen ich mich täglich umgeben möchte. Meine Produkte befriedigen insofern meine eigene Leidenschaft für Dinge, die zu meinem Leben gehören, und sicherlich auch die Leidenschaft anderer, die diese Produkte ebenfalls besitzen möchten. Es ist das gleiche wie mit der Architektur.«[14]

Richard Meier als jüdisch geprägter »White Anglo Saxon Protestant« (WASP) hat sich eine sehr spezielle Empfindsamkeit für die jüdisch grundierten Metropolen wie das Wien der Jahrhundertwende oder das Berlin der 1920er Jahre bewahrt und diese über die Jahre hinweg kultiviert. Und so atmen seine Silberobjekte für Eß- und Bürotische jene fast sakrale Eindringlichkeit und Dignität, die jüdischen Kultgeräten bis heute eigen ist. Auch hier bei diesen Silberprodukten zeigt sich wieder Meiers Vorliebe für geometrische Ornamentik. Sie alle scheinen zu sagen: »Josef Hoffmann is still alive!« Aber Meier ist in seinem Entwurfsvokabular durchaus raffinierter als beispielsweise Hoffmann oder Loos; er ist gewissermaßen durch die postmoderne Schule der Bedeutungspotenzierung gegangen, die Doppel- und Dreifachkodierungen bevorzugt. Die möglichen interpretativen Valenzen zeigen etwa seine Kerzenständer und die Silberrahmen für Photographien. Es sind geometrische Kleinskulpturen, die miniaturisierte Volumen symmetrisch oder asymmetrisch im Raum verteilen. Der Photorahmen »Ball and Column« etwa besteht aus einem rahmenlosen Doppelglas, welches auf der einen Seite bis zur halben Höhe asymmetrisch in eine kleine Silbertonne einschneidet, auf der anderen Seite in eine Kugel. Der Rahmen ruht auf einer massiven Langlochform aus Silber. Während dieser Rahmen eine klassisch-moder-

Table tops and desktop accessories

It follows its own consistency that Meier also designs glass, porcelain, and silver products for the well-set table – considering his admiration of the members of the Viennese School such as Loos, Hoffmann or Wagner. But while the geometrists of Vienna's Art Nouveau school could fall back on the Bohemian glassblowing trade, Meier's products for tables and writing desks are produced in the USA. He and many others not only American architects and designers have found an ambitious couple of producers in the New York firm of Swid Powell which has caused a sensation in the 1980s with its poduct designs, emphasizing the creative personalities and psychologies of their designers and putting them in the foreground, similar to how Alessi and Vitra did it in Europe. In the USA, it was apparently only Knoll International during the after-War decades which had followed a similar strategy. But, as has been mentioned before, this enterprise had a European character. In the area of glass, china, and silver production such a firm had long been lacking in the United States. Neither could it have been replaced by limited-issue products which were occasionally offered by galleries.Therefore, when in 1980 Nan Swid and Addie Powell founded their firm – with the first of them previously being design consultant and the second vice-president of sales in the Knoll company –, they were able to make use of that group of designers who represented at that time almost entirely the contemporary »Who is who« of the renowned, at that time of course meaning Postmodern designers: Robert Venturi, Robert A. M. Stern, Richard Meier, Stanley Tigerman and Margaret McCurry, Charles Gwathmey and Robert Siegel, Michael Graves, Steven Holl and Arquitectonica from the USA, Ettore Sottsass, George Sowden, Hans Hollein, Trix and Robert Haussmann from Europe, and Arata Isozaki from Japan. Such a phalanx of internationally renowned and also highly individualistic strategies in designing had not been assembled before in the USA since Frank Lloyd Wright and Louis Sullivan under any aspect in this kind of considered product lines.[11] Meier remarked about the initiative: »I liked Nan and Addie's enthusiasm, their naive way of saying let's make something and find out how to do it. If it weren't for their perseverance and dedication to making it work, it would have fallen apart.«[12]

Probably Paul Goldberger assesses this initiative correctly when he states: »For the architects, it was an opportunity to reestablish a link between architecture and decorative arts. Historically, architects had once been responsible for more than buildings, but not since the days of the Wiener Werkstätte, founded by Josef Hoffmann in 1903, had there been such a studio.«[13] But this statement is only applicable to the USA because in Europe, the Italian firm of Alessi has followed exactly the same path. Basically then, Swid Powell was the American response to Alessi.

If one examines Richard Meier's silver and glass products for Swid Powell, then – at least for the European-trained eye – a special »Déjavu« becomes apparent, almost like a reincarnation of the Vienna Art Nouveau, and that right in the center of Manhattan. Meier has created more than 40 products in silver for Swid Powell, about ten silver bowls and trays, a napkin holder, and a caraffe with a silver base, as well as a mini-amphora for the well-set dining table in addition to some cutlery and serving pieces. Besides these items there are his accessories for the writing desk or for the sideboard. They include frames for photographs, letter openers and containers for writing utensils, letter stands and a magnifying glass for reading, boxes for paper clips, and also book marks, money clips, and a key ring. This results in an almost complete palette of those products with which we surround ourselves in our professional or private lives considering them »personal accessories«. Four silver baptismal cups for small children were added later, also a Menorah candle holder made of polished aluminum. Meier later precisely describes the relationship between his architecture and his designs for Swid Powell as well as his motivation for these creations: »I relate these products to my architecture in that they are related to me. What I design are not only things I want to live with, but things I need. For example, I need photo frames for pictures of my children, I need bowls for nuts. I also design for Swid Powell because I haven't been able to find these things on the market that I like to live with on a daily basis. It satisfies my own particular desire for certain kinds of things that are part of life for me and for others who want them. It's the same as architecture.«[14]

Richard Meier as a »White Anglo-Saxon Protestant« (WASP) of Jewish extraction has retained a very special sentiment for the strongly Jewish-grounded metropolises such as Vienna during the turn of the century and Berlin of the 1920s and he has cultivated this sensitivity over the years. Thus, his silver objects for the dining table and the office exude this almost sacred intensity and dignity which pertains to the sacred objects of the Jewish faith right to this day. Here again, with these silver products we can observe Meier's preference for geometrical designs. They all seem to say: »Josef Hoffman is still alive!« But throughout his entire designing vocabulary, Meier is more artful than, for instance, Hoffmann or Loos. He is, indeed, influenced by the Postmodern school of increased potential meaning which prefers double and triple codes of significance. These possible interpretative valencies can be discovered, for instance, by looking at his candle holders and his silver picture frames. They respresent geometrical mini-sculptures which distribute minimized volumes arranged symmetrically or asymmetrically in the room. For example, the photo frame called »Ball and Column« consists of a frameless double glass which on its one side and up to the midpoint carves itself into a small silver drum and on the other side into a silver ball. The entire frame rests on a massive base of silver with elongated open spaces. While this particular frame possesses the grace of classical Modernism, Meier's »Ana« frame with its oval center field and its row of small, square etchings situated above alludes to more conventional forms. Other picture frames vary in their allusions to the Bauhaus and to Historism. This oscillation between different, yet always nostalgic and historical references to the

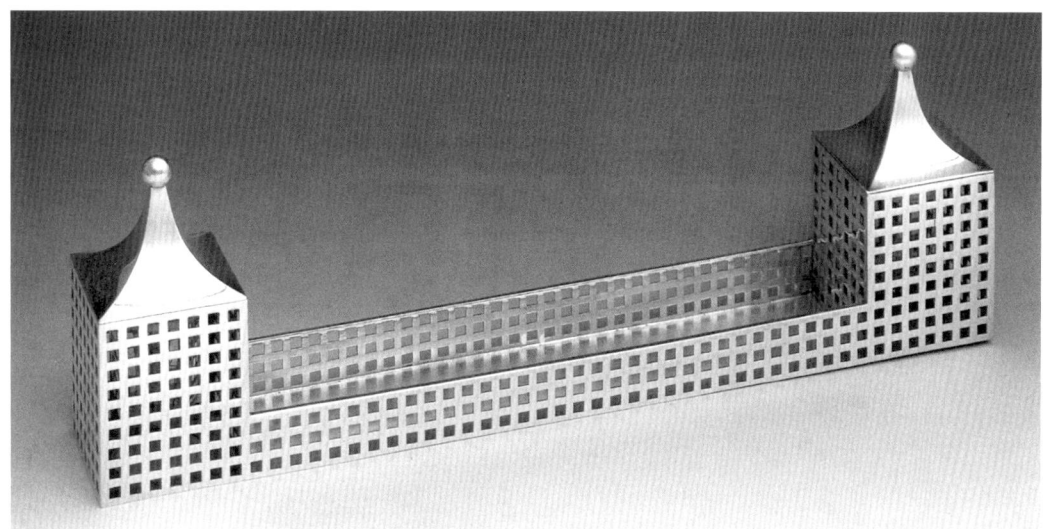

ne Anmutung hat, zeigt Meiers massiver »Ana«-Rahmen mit seinem ovalen Bildfeld und einer darüber situierten Reihe kleiner Quadrat-Stanzungen Anklänge an historische Formen. Weitere Bildträger variieren diese beiden Anspielungen an Bauhaus und Historismus. Dieses Changieren zwischen verschiedenen, gleichwohl immer leicht nostalgisch empfundenen, historischen Referenzen zwischen Gründerzeit und Bauhaus-Moderne, De Stijl und Konstruktivismus charakterisiert auch die Kerzenleuchter. Schon ihre Namen sind stilistisches Programm: »Cubist, Cylinder, Classic, Candelabra ...«. Mackintosh, Wagner, Hoffmann, Rietveld, Breuer, Malewitsch: Sie alle sind Anreger mit ihren Entwurfsvokabularien, aber eben auch nur Anreger. Denn jeder dieser Leuchter, jeder dieser Photorahmen ist trotzdem ein autonomes Werk, wohlproportioniert, stilsicher, charaktervoll. Die rektangulären Stift- und Briefklammerboxen in unterschiedlichen Größen sind mit einem quadrierten Ritznetz überzogen und stehen entweder auf kleinen Kugeln oder auf fortlaufend regelmäßig ausgestanzten Quadratreihen, was beides erneut deutlich auf Josef Hoffmann verweist, aber auch auf geometrische Banddekore sehr viel älterer, fast archaischer Zeiten. Auch die Silberschalen sind an ihren oberen Rändern durch solche durchbrochenen Quadratreihen charakterisiert. Der Briefständer fügt eine Reihe grazil dimensionierter, exakter Halbbögen auf einer Standplatte aneinander und empfiehlt sich so durchaus auch als toasttauglich. Den Brieföffner, den Buchclip, den Schlüsselring und den Geldscheinhalter kennzeichnen wie ein durchgehendes »Logo« vier zu einem Quadrat angeordnete ausgestanzte Quadrate. Auch Meiers Bestecke, ob für Swid Powell oder für Reed & Barton, wirken mit ihren langzinkigen Gabeln, den auf Kreisen oder Querellipsen aufgebauten Löffeln und Kellen sowie den Messern, deren Schneiden Hyperbelformen folgen, wie eine abstrahierend-ferne Erinnerung an den geometrischen Jugendstil Wiener Prägung. Ihr systematischer Formenaufbau ist von exakter Strenge gekennzeichnet: mathematische Exerzitien! Und wiederum gibt es – in Cloisonné-Technik eingelegte – verzierende, kleine Quadratreihen, die auch die Bestecke und Vorlege-Bestecke stilistisch und persönlich positionieren – »signature grid patterns«. Verschiedene Hoffmann-Produkte verdeutlichen die Bezüge.

Bei seinem Porzellandekor »Signature« für Swid Powell hat Meier seine Vorliebe für geometrisches Dekor geradezu auf die Spitze getrieben. Die reinweißen Tassen und Teller werden jeweils durch ein strichdünnes Fadenkreuz geviertelt: eine lapidare Geste der Durchstreichung von Form, die an dem ontologischen Radikalismus vieler Minimalisten geschult erscheint. Keine formbegleitende Ornamentik also, kein den Schwüngen, Radien und Rundformen schmeichelndes Dekor. Selbst wenn man die Speisen sensibel in den Begrenzungen der Viertelkreise positionieren würde, bliebe die artifizielle Formzerstörung erhalten, ja würde noch betont. Und wenn sich bei runden Tellern ein Strichnetz über die Diagonale zur Mitte hin kontinuierlich, aber asymmetrisch auflöst, dann hat das nicht zuletzt den Charakter einer Skizze, wobei der Wert der »graphischen Unfertigkeit« ja seinerseits historisch kodiert ist.

Andererseits hat Meier auch durchaus eher gefällige, formbegleitende und -betonende Dekore entworfen, die erneut auf die Wiener Schule, manchmal auch auf die Glasgower Schule von Mackintosh verweisen. So beziehen sich viele eingebrannte Glasuren oder auch dreidimensionale Quadratreihen weiß-in-weiß auf die architektonische Ornamentik der Jahrhundertwende – auf Möbel um 1900. Auch die Form der Volumen ist eher architektonisch aufgefaßt: Zum Beispiel sind fast alle Tassenformen dieses Entwerfers prinzipiell hochzylindrische Volumen und vermeiden die flach und breit gelagerte Charakteristik von Teeschalen. Zudem spricht es für die formale Disziplin Meiers, daß er auch bei der Verwendung »minimalistischer« Dekore niemals den Bezug zu den Volumen der Gefäße negiert.

Auch Meiers Kristallglas-Kollektion für Swid Powell ist in weiten Teilen Josef Hoffmann verpflichtet. Das fängt bei den Formen und Formaten an und setzt sich bei der gewählten Ornamentik fort. Drei der fünf verschiedenen Trinkgläser, eine Schale und zwei Vasen haben geätzte Strichdekore. Die formbegleitenden, d.h. formbetonenden Parallelätzungen legen sich wie grazile Drahtgitter um die Glasvolumen, die damit stilistisch historisiert werden. Assoziationen an den Prager Jugendstil oder den Wiener Koloman Moser stellen sich ein. Doch leistet sich Meier auch »freie« Ätzdekore, die fast wie zufällige Kratzer aussehen. Zwei weitere Trinkgläser und

1. Josef Hoffmann, Tintenfässer und Schreibtischablage, um 1905; Josef Wagner.
2. Josef Hoffmann, Teile eines 106teiligen Bestecks für 12 Personen, 1904–08.
3. Josef Hoffmann, zwei Gläser und eine Karaffe, um 1920; Lobmeyr.
4. Josef Hoffmann, »Vide-Poche«, um 1904.

1. Josef Hoffmann, inkpots and desk set, c. 1905; Josef Wagner.
2. Josef Hoffmann, parts of a cutlery of 106 pieces for 12 persons, 1904–08.
3. Josef Hoffmann, two glasses and a decanter, c. 1920; Lobmeyr.
4. Josef Hoffmann, »Vide-Poche«, c. 1904.

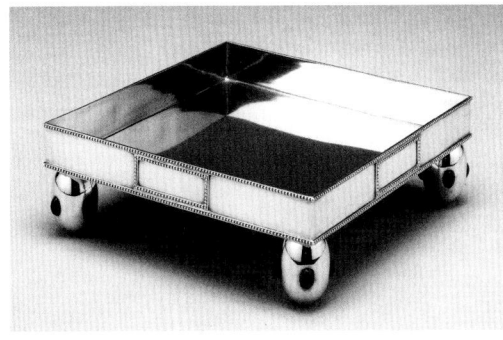

late 19th century or Bauhaus Modernism, the De Stijl movement and Constructivism also characterize the candlesticks. Already the names indicate a stylistic program, such as »Cubist, Cylinder, Classic, Candelabra ...«. Macintosh, Wagner, Hoffmann, Rietveld, Breuer, Malewitsch, they have all been stimulators for this program with their vocabularies of design, but they have been no more than that. Each of the candelabra, each one of the picture frames is, after all, an autonomous creation, well proportioned and stylistically full of character. The rectangular box containers of varying sizes for writing implements and for paper clips are covered by a quadratic grille of engravings. They stand either on small ball shapes or on rows of etched squares arranged in continuous sequence, both being references to Josef Hoffmann. At the same time, there seems to be a reference to ribbon decorations of a much older and almost archaic era. The silver bowls as well are characterized by such opened-square rows of decorations. For instance, on the letter stand a row of gracefully dimensioned, perfect semi-circles is interconnected and, thus, becomes useful in the unforeseen function as a toast holder. In the same way, the letter opener, the bookmark, the key ring, and the money clip are characterized by such a continuous »logo«, here in the arrangement of four hollowed and sequencial squares which come together in one large square. Meier's cutlery, whether for Swid Powell or for Reed & Barton, also brings back distant and abstracting memories of the Art Nouveau of Viennese coinage considering their long-toothed forks, their spoons and ladles incorporating circles and cross-ellipses, or their knives whose cutting blades follow the outlines of hyperboles. Their systematic formal design is characterized by exact precision, akin to mathematical exercises! Here again, there are those small ornamental rows of squares, inlaid and executed in Cloisonné technique. They are the same which make a personal and stylistic position statement with the cutlery and serving pieces and their »signature grid patterns«. Some pieces by Hoffmann may explain these connections.

Meier has almost gone to the extreme in his preference for geometrical ornamentation on his porcelain called »Signature«. Cups and plates in pure white are each sectioned in four quarters through a fine line crossing: a lapidary gesture which signifies the crossing-out of form as it could be understood from the aspect of ontological radicalism of many Minimalists. Here, there is no ornamentation, such as curves, radii, or any other decoration which might flatter the round shape of the outline. Even if one would be determined attempting to put menu items inside the borderlines of the quarter segments of these dishes, the artificial destruction of the intra-lineal form would remain; it might even be stressed further. And if on the round plates a net of lines continually, but asymmetrically dissolves across their diagonal line towards the center where it disappears, then this finally creates the effect of a sketch; the validity of the »graphical incompleteness«, however, being in itself historically codified.

On the other hand, Meier has created an attractive ornamentation which accompanies the form of the individual products almost throughout, which again refers back to the Viennese School and also, at times to the Glasgow School of Mackintosh. In the same way, many baked-in finishes or three-dimensional rows of white-in-white squares take refence to the architectural ornaments of the turn of the century, especially to furnishings around 1900. Even the shape of the volumes is taken in a rather architectural way. For instance and as a matter of principle, almost all cups of this designer use a high, cylindrical volume and avoid the flat and wide shape which is otherwise characteristic of teacups or bowls. It also speaks for the formative discipline of Meier when he uses Minimalistic ornamental patterns, but never leaves the relationship of the decoration to the volume of these dishes out of consideration.

Even Meier's crystal-glass collection for Swid Powell draws largely on Josef Hoffmann. This begins with the designs and formats and continues towards the decorations. Three of the five drinking glasses, one bowl, and two vases have etched linear ornaments. The etchings of parallel lines which follow the outline of the glass volumes and underline its exterior form, drape themselves around the glass shapes like a graceful wire mesh, giving the object the appearance of a historical style. This image creates associations with the Art Nouveau of Prague or with Koloman Moser of Vienna. But Meier also permits himself »free«, decorative etchings which almost have the appearance of unintentional skratches. But two other drinking glasses and a carafe for wine with a glass prop are plain and refer, like the glass bowls which Meier has designed for the Steuben Group and the ceramic objects for the Swedish company Arabia, to the pure material and the pure form. Even this concept pays tribute to Modernism, but maybe more to that of Skandinavia and the work of Alvar Aalto. Meier's undecorated glass products with their rims in dull polish are elegant, organical containers. The mere thickness of the material produces lively and reflecting interior figuration, even without applied ornaments. A small cylindrical container of oval outlines and covered by a silver lid may be used for precious liquids or partly luiquid ingredients such as, maybe, English bitter marmelade. In that regard, this concept of design may also represent the author's esteem for the British Wedgwood culture which has celebrated such essences on dining tables since the turn of the century. One can see that Richard Meier is interested throughout in the culture of dining in the traditional sense and, without embarrassment, makes use of the historically developed dining implements which are among the fine products and product lines that were developed in England, France, Germany, or Austria during the time which, after all, was named the »Belle Epoque«. Any elegant household around 1890, be it in Vienna or London, in Paris, or Berlin had, along with its maybe ten to twelve family members equally as many servants. There usually was also a very large kitchen with several cooks, and there were waitresses for the dining room and additonal domestic staff. China sets containing more than 200 pieces, for more than 30 special functions were quite common in such circles. Au temps perdu! The cultural philosopher Arnold Gehlen once desribed this situation:

eine Weinkaraffe mit Glasverschluß sind dagegen glatt und setzen wie die gläsernen Schalen, die Meier für die Steuben Group und die Keramikteile, welche er für das schwedische Unternehmen Arabia entworfen hat, ausschließlich auf das pure Material und die reine Form: Auch das ist eine Reverenz an die Moderne, allerdings mehr an die skandinavische, vielleicht an jene von Alvar Aalto. Meiers ornamentlose Glasprodukte mit stumpf geschliffenem Rand sind elegante, organische Behälter. Die schiere Materialstärke ergibt auch ohne applizierte Ornamentik eine lebendige, spiegelnde Binnenzeichnung. Ein kleines ovales Zylindergefäß mit Silberdeckel mag für edle flüssige oder halbflüssige Ingredienzien wie etwa englische Bittermarmelade dienen: Insofern ist dies dann auch eine Reverenz an die britische Wedgwood-Kultur, die solche Essenzen auf dem gedeckten Tisch seit Jahrhunderten zelebriert. Man sieht: Richard Meier ist es um Tafelkultur durchaus im traditionellen Sinne zu tun, und er bedient sich fast ungeniert des historisch entwickelten Instrumentariums der verfeinerten Produkte und Produktgattungen, die England, Frankreich, Deutschland und Österreich in der nicht zuletzt auch deshalb so genannten »Belle Epoque« entwickelten. Ein herrschaftlicher Haushalt um 1890 etwa, ob in Wien oder London, Paris oder Berlin, hatte bei vielleicht zehn oder zwölf Familienmitgliedern ebenso viele Hausangestellte, eine Riesenküche mit mehreren Köchen, Serviermädchen für das Eßzimmer und weitere zahlreiche Dienstboten. Porzellanservice mit mehr als 200 Teilen für mehr als 30 spezielle Funktionen waren in solchen Kreisen durchaus üblich. Au temps perdu! Der Kulturphilosoph Arnold Gehlen schrieb einmal darüber: »Es war eine Zeit, in der der Alltag noch von Sonn- und Feiertagen deutlich getrennt war. Man lebte gewissermaßen ›durchgegriffener‹ als heute.«¹⁵

Meiers Tisch- und Schreibtischprodukte sind insgesamt, ob in Silber, Porzellan oder Glas, Versprechen für und Erinnerung an eine Epoche, in der, wie kultursoziologisch herausgearbeitet wurde, »die sozialen Klassenunterschiede zwischen ›oben‹ und ›unten‹ noch weitgehend unbezweifelbar waren«. Die Dignität und selbstverständliche Eleganz dieser Gebrauchsprodukte sind ihnen gewissermaßen gestaltpsychologisch und materialästhetisch zugleich von vornherein eingeschrieben: Sie bedürfen insofern weder der heute grassierenden Siebdruck-Veredelungsstrategie auf industriellem Preßglas noch der pop-kulturellen Spaßstrategie mancher Küchenkreationen italienischer Prägung; und schon gar nicht bedürfen sie der semitransparenten oder grellbunten Farbigkeit jener »Lifestyle«- und »Wellness«-Accessoires, die weltweit die Küchen- und Badabteilungen der Kaufhäuser dominieren.

Für Meier selbst, und wohl auch für die Käufer seiner Produkte, sind diese den Alltag nobilitierenden Gegenstände eine nostalgische Verbeugung nicht ohne leichte Wehmut gegenüber einer Zeit, in der solche Produkte noch selbstverständlich auch den Alltag kulturell unterfütterten. Mit hoher ästhetischer Kompetenz das Feld der »domestic landscapes« zu bestellen, bedeutet nichts weniger als die Nobilitierung des Banalen. Die stilistische Durchdringung und die formgeschichtliche Zuspitzung sowie die definierte Positionierung sind immer ein Zeichen von Qualität, unabhängig von Stilfragen, Stilvorlieben oder bloßem Geschmack. Auch die »stummen Diener« (Dieter Rams) können gehaltvoll sein.

Am eindrucksvollsten hat Meier diese stilistische Durchdringung in einem äußerst anspruchsvollen Projekt für Alessi realisiert. 1983 initiierte Alessandro Mendini für dieses italienische Unternehmen eine Serie von ausdrucksstarken postmodernen »Liebhaberobjekten« aus Sterlingsilber, die »Tea and Coffee Piazzas«. Zu den eingeladenen 13 Entwerfern gehörten Michael Graves, Aldo Rossi, Oscar Tusquets, Hans Hollein, Stanley Tigerman, Arata Isozaki, Charles Jencks und Richard Meier. Mendini sah die Notwendigkeit, »gespalten zwischen der Verantwortung gegenüber Tradition und der Faszination, die vom Unbekannten ausging«, zu den Anfängen der Architekten-Produktentwürfe der 50er Jahre zurückzukehren, als die »reinen« Formen besonders wichtig waren. Bei allen Entwürfen handelt es sich um Kaffee- und Teekannen, Zucker- und Milchbehälter, die jeweils auf einem runden, ovalen oder auch in unregelmäßigen Freiformen konturiertem Tablett positioniert werden. Vorgabe war, daß die Entwerfer die Position des einzelnen Gefäßes analog der Positionierung von Gebäuden auf oder um einen Platz definierten oder fixierten. Richard Meier hat ein komplexes Zusammenwirken kubischer und bauchiger Körper erdacht, die sich in einem im doppelten Sinne des Wortes glänzenden Wechselspiel durchdringen und Innen und Außen, Behälter und Inhalt dialektisch verbinden. Die Durchdringung der Volumen zeigt einen dramatischen, fast zerklüfteten Charakter: Die Geometrie wird durch Winkelverschiebungen und Achsenverschneidungen lebendig. Theoretisch kann man dies als subkutane Barockisierung platonischer Körper und ihrer mathematischen Regelmäßigkeiten beschreiben. Vor allem die beiden Kannen erinnern an konstruktivistische Skulpturen und an ein suprematistisches Teeservice von Kasimir Malewitsch aus Porzellan (1918). Dessen asymmetrisch abgeflachte Tasse entspricht Meiers Milchkännchen, die Parallelepipede der Kannenkörper aus prismatisch zerklüfteten Volumen erscheinen verwandt, ebenso Kannengriffe und Deckel. Für Meier aber sind solche Anregungen Anlaß eigenständiger Erfindungen, weitaus komplexer, genauer, auch ambitionierter als die »Bilder im Kopf«. Meiers Alessi-»Piazza« ist gerade in der Transzendierung und zugleich Fortschreibung einer formalen Matrix eines der prominentesten Beispiele einer historisch sensiblen wie zeitgenössisch avancierten ästhetischen Kraft, die Anregung in Aufregung übersetzt. Brüche, Härten, scharfe Kontraste sind da nicht nur gewollt, sondern für den Entwurf konstituierend. Aber sie werden ausponderiert, in einer spannungsvollen Balance gehalten, und: sie statuieren, fast störrisch, einen beträchtlichen ästhetischen Eigensinn, der das bloße Servieren von Tee oder Kaffee zu einer kulturellen Zelebration überhöht. Die »Tea and Coffee Piazzas« sind das sicherlich renommierteste Design-Forschungsprojekt der »Officina Alessi«, die Gebrauchsgegenstände für den gedeckten Tisch als exklusive Multiples zelebrieren: Jedes der »Piazza«-Objekte wurde limitiert in einer Auflage von 99 Exemplaren hergestellt und kostet ca. 25 000 Euro. Zusätzlich gibt es jeweils drei »Artists Proofs«.

5. Kasimir Malewitsch, Teeservice, 1918.
6. 7. Richard Meier, »Tea and Coffee Piazza«, 1983; Alessi Spa., Crusinallo di Omega, Italien.

5. Kazimir Malevich, tea service, 1918.
6. 7. Richard Meier, »Tea and Coffee Piazza«, 1983; Alessi Spa., Crusinallo di Omega, Italy.

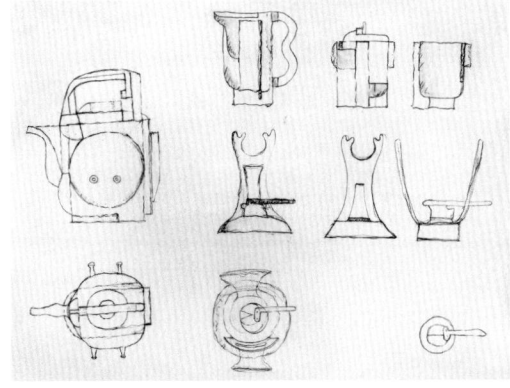

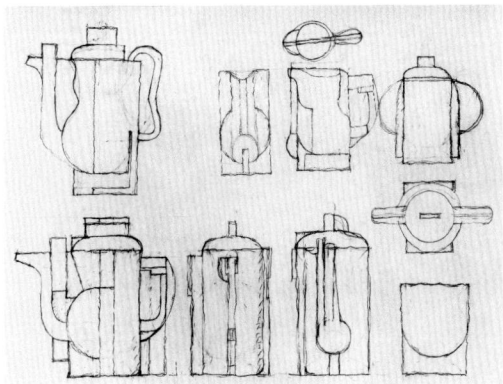

»Once, there was a time when workdays were distinctly separated from sun- and festive days. One lived, so to speak ›more uncompromisingly‹ than today.«[15]

Meier's products for the dining table and the writing desk are overall promises for an epoch and remembrances of another in which – according to socio-cultural consideratons – »the social class distinctions between ›upper‹ and ›lower‹ were overall still quite clearly understood«. This is to say that the dignity and the natural elegance of these household items are innate to them from the start and whether one looks at them from an aspect of form psychology or considers them from the angle of an estheticism of the material. In this respect, they neither need the »refinement« process of screen printing on industrial pressed glass which is common today, nor do they require the fun strategies based in Pop culture and found with some kitchen products of Italian background, nor even the semi-transparent or garish coloring of those »lifestyle« or »wellness accessories«, which dominate the kitchen and bath sections of department stores worldwide.

For Meier himself and certainly for the buyers of his products, these creations which somehow ennoble our everyday life spread a nostalgic reverence and contain a certain melancholy towards a by-gone time in which such implements still culturally enriched the workday with self-evidence. To enrich the fields of the »domestic landscape« with high esthetical competency means no less than to render a certain nobility to the otherwise banal. Stylistic pervasion and form-historical accentuation as well as distinct positioning always set a sign of quality, independent from questions about style in general, about stylistic preferences, or just about mere good taste. According to the words of Dieter Rams, even the »silent butlers« can be important.

Meier has realized this understanding of style especially well in a rather ambitious project for Alessi. In 1983, Alessandro Mendini initiated for this Italian company a series of impressive Postmodern »objects for enthusiasts«, the »Tea and Coffee Piazzas« in sterling silver. Among the 13 invited designers were Michael Graves, Aldo Rossi, Oscar Tusquets, Hans Hollein, Stanley Tigerman, Arata Isozaki, Charles Jencks, and Richard Meier. Mendini saw that it was necessary to return to the architectural product designs of the 1950s when »pure« forms were especially en vogue. But he was also aware of the »dichotomy between a responsibility towards tradition and a fascination for the unknown«. All the designs pertain to such objects as coffee and teapots and sugar and milk servers each of which is positioned on a round, oval, or even irregularly free-shaped serving tray. The designers were to define or determine exactly the position of each dish in analogous relationship to buildings on or around a piazza. Richard Meier invented a complex scheme of integrated containers with cubic and bulbous bodies which interrelate splendidly with each other. In the dialectial sense of the word, they also meld interior and exterior, container and contents. The fusion of the volumes shows a dramatic and almost abruptly fissured character. The geometry is enlivened through a shifting of the angles and a dissecting of the axes. In theory, one could describe this as subcutaneous adaptation of Platonic bodies to style elements of the Baroque era and to their mathematical regularities. Especially the two coffee and teapots remind of Constructivist sculptures and possibly also of a Suprematistic tea set of porcelain by Kazimir Malevich (1918). Here, the assymmetrically flattened cup corresponds with Meier's milk dispenser, the parallelepipede of the pot bodies which consists of cragged prisms appears to be related to other objects by Malevich, also the handles of the pots and the lids. For Meier, these stimulations through others always give rise to his own new inventions, extensively more complex, more exact, and more ambitious than the »mental images«. By transcending and, at the same time, further developing the formal matrix, Meier's Alessi »Piazza« is one of the most prominent examples of a historically sensitive and an advanced esthetical effort in our time which translates stimulus into excitement. Here, cracks or fissures, harshness, or sharp contrasts are not only intended, but they constitute part of the design. Meanwhile, all of these are carefully considered and the tension of the total design is kept in balance. Additionally, the items declare in an almost stern determination a major esthetical independence which transforms the mere serving of tea or coffee into a cultural celebration. The »Tea and Coffee Piazzas« constitute most certainly the most renowned research project in the field of design which has been issued by the »Officina Alessi«. The project elevates household implements for the well set dining table to something exclusively diverse and unusual. Each of the »Piazza« objects was issued in a limited production of 99 pieces and at a cost of approximately 25 000 Euro. There also exist three additional »artist proofs« each.

1. »Tea and Coffee Piazza«, 1983; Alessi Spa.,
Crusinallo di Omega, Italien.
2. Kerzenleuchter »Tower«, 1986, »Candelabra«,
1984, »Classic«, 1984, und »Cylinder«, 1988, sowie Vase »Bud«, 1988; Swid Powell, New York.

1. »Tea and Coffee Piazza«, 1983. Alessi Spa.,
Crusinallo di Omega, Italy.
2. »Tower« candlestick, 1986, »Candelabra«
candlestick, 1984, »Classic« candlestick, 1984,
»Cylinder« candlestick, 1988, and »Bud« vase,
1988; Swid Powell, New York.

3. Serviettenring, 1995, zwei Babytassen, 1995, Pfeffermühle, 1986, und Salzstreuer, 1986; Swid Powell, New York.
4. Zwei Krüge, Anfang der 1990er Jahre; Swid Powell, New York.

3. Napkin ring, 1995, two baby cups, 1995, peppermill, 1986, and salt shaker, 1986; Swid Powell, New York.
4. Two pitchers, early 1990s; Swid Powell, New York.

5. Kleine Schale, 1985, große Schale, 1985, und Konfektschale, 1986; Swid Powell, New York.
6. Ovales Tablett, 1984, Speisenschale auf Sockel (Schale, Deckel, Glasschale), 1986, und Schale auf Sockel, 1985; Swid Powell, New York.

5. Cross bowl, 1985, large bowl, 1985, and candy dish, 1986; Swid Powell, New York.
6. Tray oval, 1984, pedestal dish set (bowl, lid, glass dish), 1986, and pedestal bowl, 1985; Swid Powell, New York.

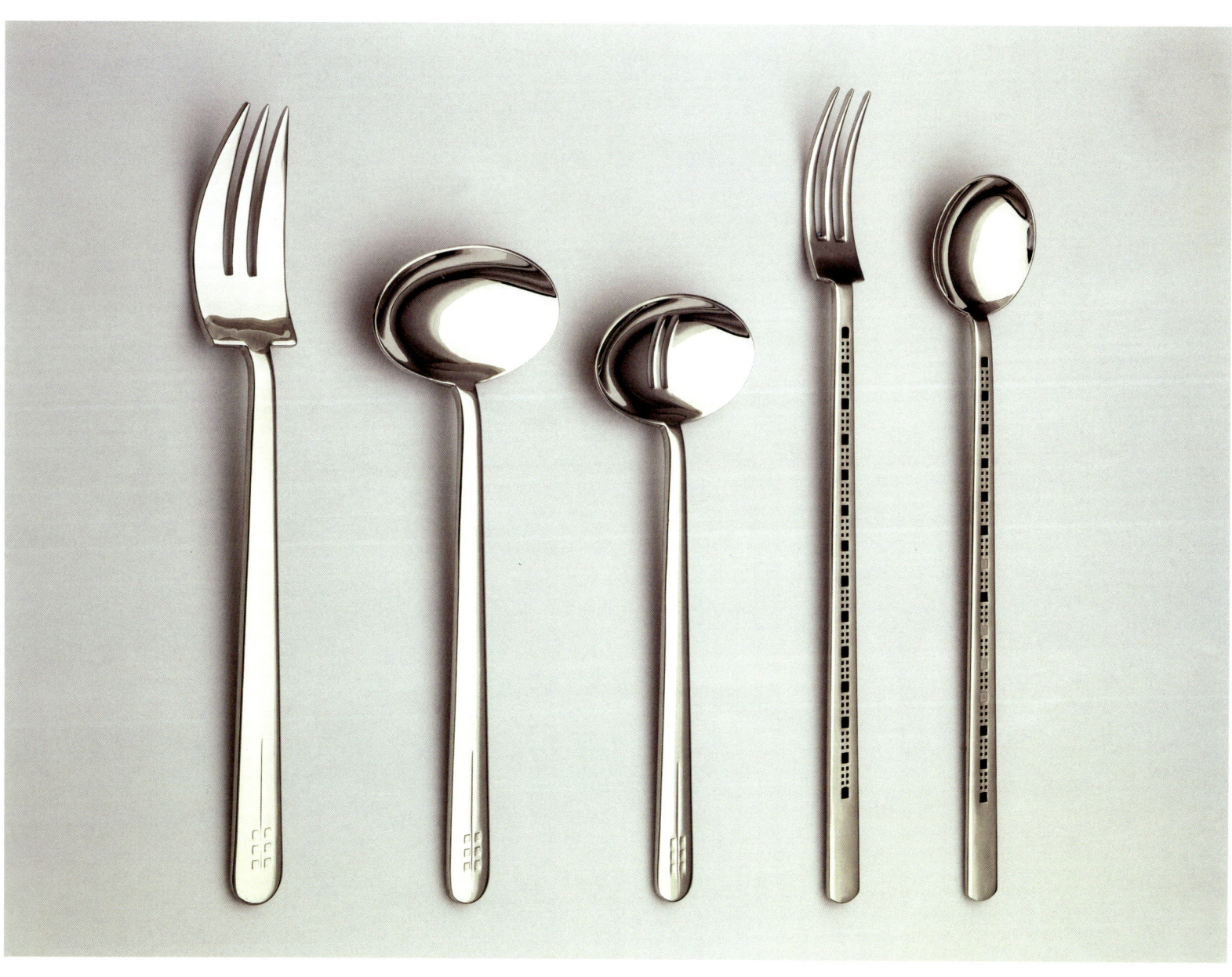

7. Vorlegegabel, 1992, Vorlegelöffel, 1991, und Vorlegelöffel mit Schlitzen, 1992; Reed & Barton, Taunton, USA. Salatbesteck mit Email-Einlagen, Ende 1980er Jahre; Swid Powell, New York.
8. Buttermesser, Messer, Gabel, Salatgabel, Suppenlöffel, Dessertlöffel und Teelöffel, 1991; Reed & Barton, Taunton, USA.

7. Large serving fork, 1992, large serving spoon, 1991, and large serving spoon with slots, 1992; Reed & Barton, Taunton, USA. Salad serving fork and salad serving spoon with enamel inlay, late 1980s; Swid Powell, New York.
8. Butter knife, dinner knife, dinner fork, salad fork, soup spoon, dessert spoon, and tea spoon, 1991; Reed & Barton, Taunton, USA.

42

9. Briefständer, 1984, Brieföffner, 1984, und Zuckerdose, 1991; Swid Powell, New York.
10. Lesezeichen, 1985, Vergrößerungsglas, 1986, und Tablett, 1985; Swid Powell, New York.

9. Letter rack, 1985, letter opener, 1984, and sugar bowl, 1991; Swid Powell, New York.
10. Bookmark, 1985, magnifying glass, 1986, and tray medium, 1985; Swid Powell, New York.

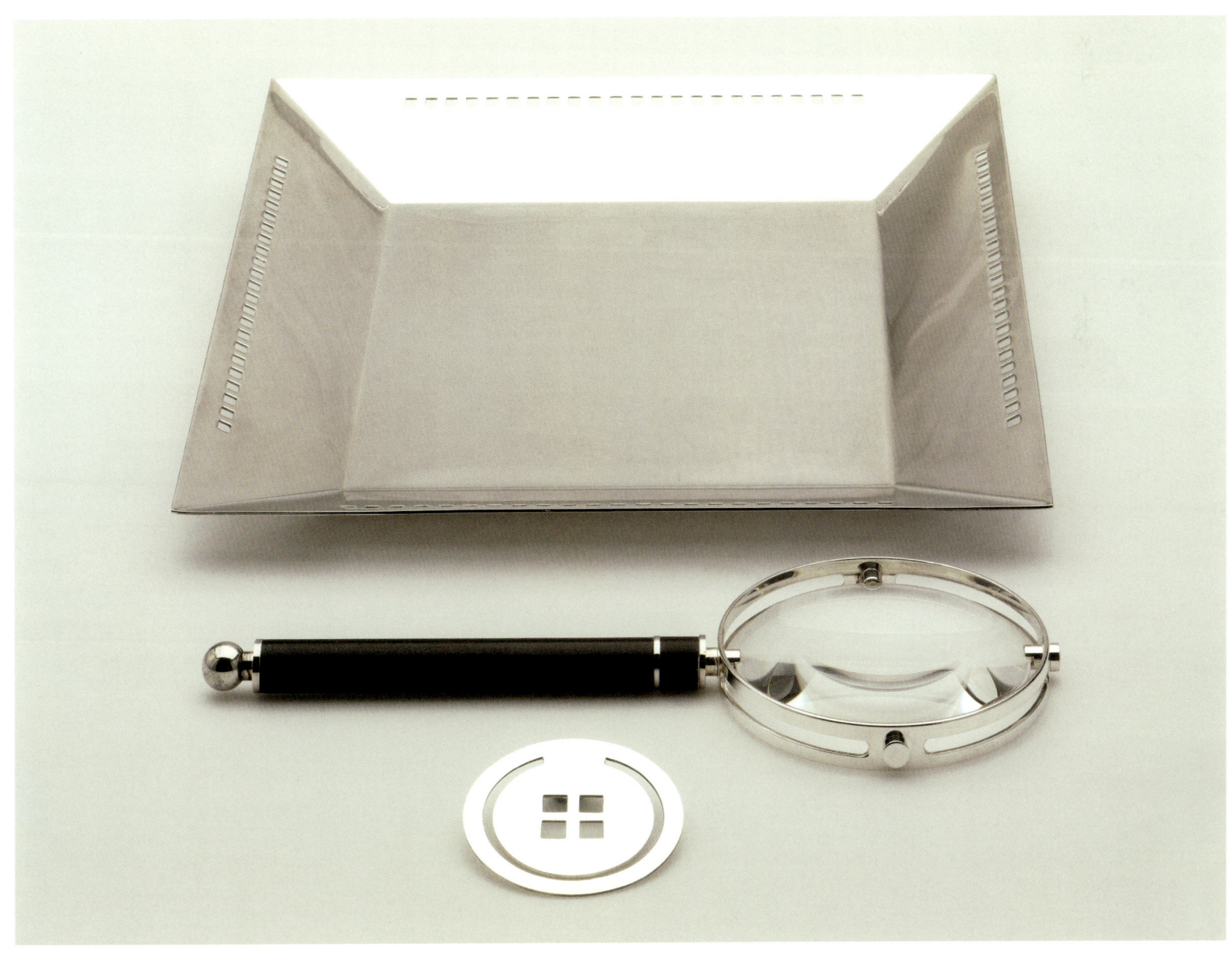

11. Stiftständer, 1984, kleines Tablett, 1985, Heftklammerbox, 1987; Swid Powell, New York.
12. Photoschachtel, 1989, Photorahmen mit Säule »Ana«, 1986, und kleiner Photorahmen, 1987; Swid Powell, New York.
13. Photorahmen mit Säule, 1986, Rahmen mit Glaseinsatz, 1987, und kleiner Rahmen »Ana«, 1986, Swid Powell, New York.

11. Pencil cup, 1984, small tray, 1985, and medium box, 1987; Swid Powell, New York.
12. Frame Box, 1989, »Ana« column frame, 1986, and small frame, 1987; Swid Powell, New York.
13. Column frame, 1986, frame with glas insert, 1987, small »Ana« frame, 1986; Swid Powell, New York.

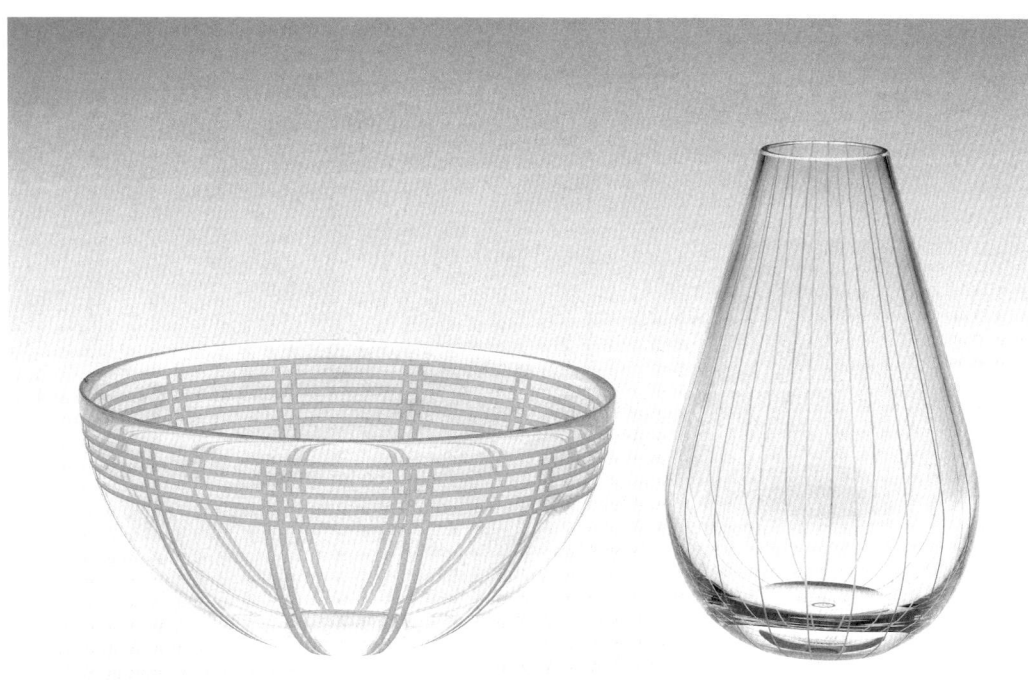

14. Karaffe mit Deckel »Grid« und Vase »Manhattan«, Anfang der 1990er Jahre; Swid Powell, New York.
15. Vase »Lattice« und Vase »Linear«, Anfang der 1990er Jahre; Swid Powell, New York.
16. Hohes Trinkglas »Grid«, niedriges Trinkglas »Grid«, Wasserglas mit Sockel, Glas »Goblet« und Trinkglas »Manhattan«, Anfang der 1990er Jahre; Swid Powell, New York.
17. Ovale Glasschale mit Holzdeckel (Zucker), verschiedene offene Glasschalen, 1992; Steuben Glass, New York.

14. »Grid« decanter with lid, and »Manhattan« vase, early 1990s; Swid Powell, New York.
15. »Lattice« and »Linear« vases, early 1990s; Swid Powell, New York.
16. »Grid« high glass, »Grid« low glass, pedestal water glass, »Goblet« footed glass, »Manhattan« glass, early 1990s; Swid Powell, New York.
17. Oval glass bowl with wood lid (sugar), various open bowls, 1992; Steuben Glass, New York.

18. Teller, Dessertteller, Tasse und Untertasse »Signature black«, 1984; Swid Powell, New York.
19. Suppenteller und Untertasse »Signature black«, 1984; Swid Powell, New York.

18. »Signature black« buffet plate, dessert plate, cup, and saucer, 1984; Swid Powell, New York.
19. »Signature black« soup bowl and saucer, 1984; Swid Powell, New York.

20. Servierteller, Suppenteller, Tasse und Untertasse »Signature«, 1984; Swid Powell, New York.
21. Tasse, Untertasse und Dessertteller »Meier White« 1991/92, sowie Dessertteller, Tasse und Untertasse »Grid«, 1992; Swid Powell, New York.

20. »Signature« serving bowl, soup bowl, cup, and saucer, 1984; Swid Powell, New York.
21. »Meier White« cup, saucer and dessert plate, 1991/1992, and »Grid« dessert plate, cup and saucer, 1992; Swid Powell, New York.

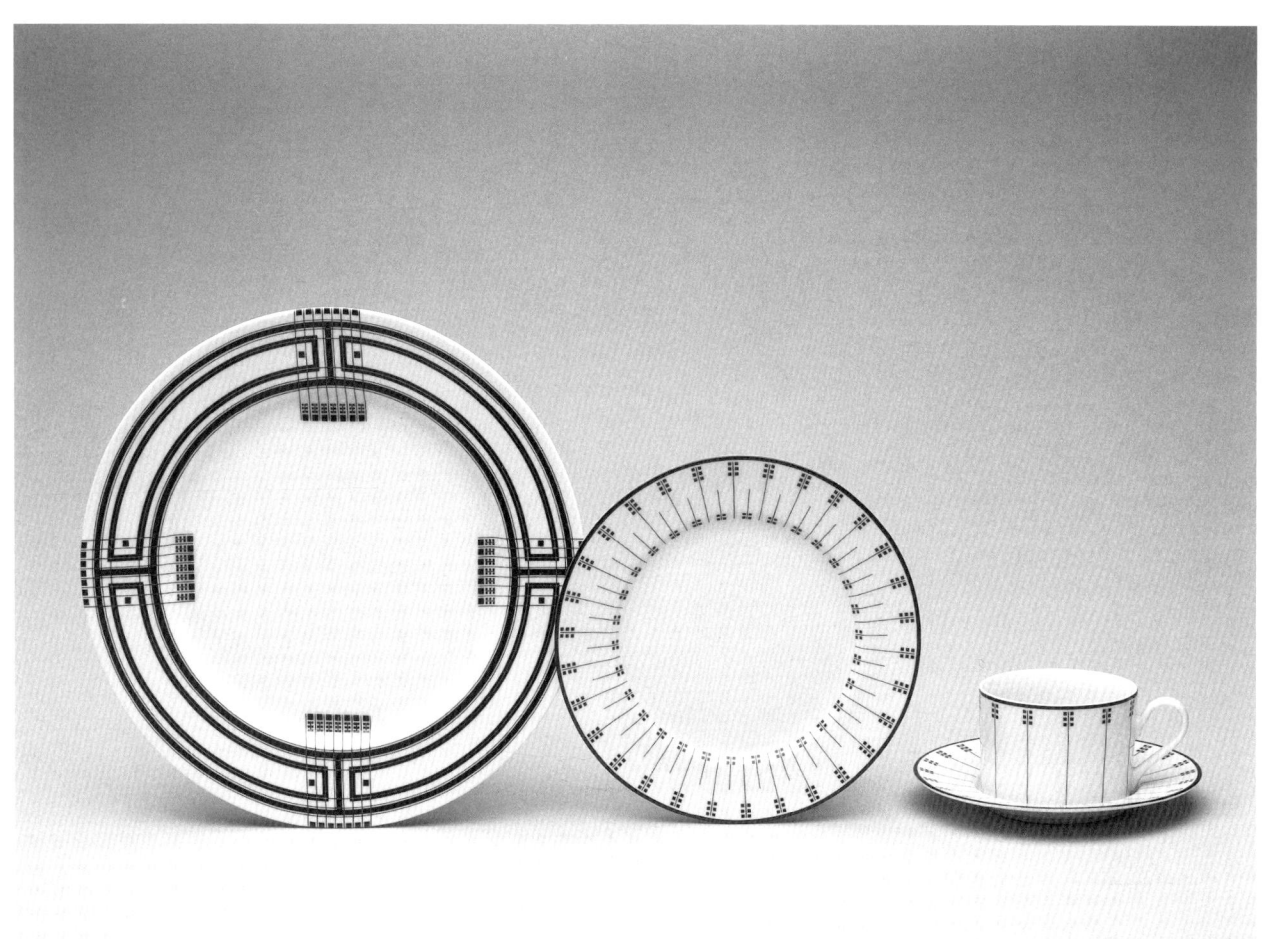

22. Eßteller »Metropol« und Dessertteller, Tasse, und Untertasse »Ray«, Anfang der 1990er Jahre; Swid Powell, New York.
23. Teller »Ray«, Anfang der 1990er Jahre sowie Zuckerdose und Milchkännchen »Meier White«, 1991/92; Swid Powell, New York.
24. Weiße Trinkbecher mit dunkelblauen Streifen und Eierbecher »Space Collection«, 2000; Arabia, Stockholm.
25. Teller, Schüssel, und Unterteller »Space Collection«, 2000; Arabia, Stockholm, Schweden.
26. Teller und Unterteller »Space Collection«, 2000; Arabia, Stockholm.

22. »Metropol« dinner plate and »Ray« dessert plate, cup and saucer, early 1990s; Swid Powell, New York.
23. »Ray« plate, early 1990s, and »Meier White« sugar and creamer, 1991/92; Swid Powell, New York.
24. »Space collection« white mugs with dark blue stripe and egg cup, 2000; Arabia, Stockholm.
25. »Space collection« plate, bowl and saucer, 2000; Arabia, Stockholm.
26. »Space collection« plates and saucer, 2000; Arabia, Stockholm.

Persönliche Accessoires

Ab 1982 beauftragte der italienische Hersteller Cleto Munari etwa 15 führende zeitgenössische Architekten und Designer, echten Schmuck zu entwerfen. Neben den Postmodernen Robert Venturi, Stanley Tigerman, Robert A. M. Stern und Arata Isozaki gehörten auch die Neomodernen Ettore Sottsass und Alessandro Mendini sowie Mario Bellini und Richard Meier zu den Designern.

Meier kreierte 1985 zwei Ringe, die jeweils aus 18 Karat Gold und schwarzem und weißem Onyx bestehen. Einer der Ringe ist ein fast klassisch-konservativer dreigeteilter Reif, der sich an den Unterteilungen jeweils verdickt und als »Füllung« eine umlaufende Reihe schwarzer und weißer Felder aufweist. Damit bekommt er den Charakter einer Sakralfassade der Frührenaissance. Der zweite Ring dagegen ist deutlich asymmetrisch. Aus ihm wachsen in Form eines senkrecht zum Finger stehenden Viertelkreises unterschiedlich dimensionierte Onyxsegmente, aneinandergesetzte Trapeze, wiederum an Bossensteine von Renaissance-Palästen erinnernd. Diese »tanzenden« Formen, Borromini- oder Alberti-Details nachempfunden, mit den rational-labyrinthischen Raumdurchdringungen von Meiers Architektursprache korrespondierend, fügen ihm aber eine über die Reverenz an die 1920er Jahre weiter zurückreichende historische Allusion hinzu. Oder wird hier der Schwarz-Weiß-Schmuck des Wiener Jugendstils à la Otto Wagner konterkarierend zitiert? Jene Schwarz-Weiß-Kompartimente mag man aber auch als Hinweis auf die, hier buchstäblich aus den Fugen geratene, Ratio eines Schachbretts oder die rhythmische Abfolge von Klaviertasten lesen.

Meiers Armbanduhren für das Unternehmen Markuse nehmen sich dagegen formal erneut zurück. Die Herren-Chronometer zeichnen sich durch klassisch-runde Zifferblätter aus. Auf ihrem ziffernlosen Rand dominieren die eleganten Stunden- und Minutenzeiger sowie Meiers handschriftliche Signatur. Die Zeit wird mithin jeweils nur annähernd gemessen. Die zeitgenössischen Exaktheitsphobien etwa bei sportlichen Wettkämpfen werden damit zurückgewiesen. Mit den Worten Arnold Gehlens: »Es geht ... um den Ekel vor einer Welt, in der man mit Hundertstelsekunden belästigt wird, mit Katastrophen im Sonstwoland, mit Hochrechnungen und mit einem Bombardement von Forderungen, Ratschlägen und Warnungen. Jeder Berufszweig ... wird angenörgelt, und Roboter taumeln auf dem Mond herum.«[16]

Solche analogen, gewissermaßen »klassische« Herrenarmbanduhren unterliegen naturgemäß weniger modischen Strömungen als ihre femininen Pendants und widersprechen technisch hochgerüsteten Astronauten-, Aquanauten- und Flugkapitän-Chronometern, vorzugsweise mit 15 bis 20 Zusatzfunktionen. Solche »engineer watches« haben oft noch zusätzlich drehbare Außenringe ums Zifferblatt mit Kompaß- oder nautischen Kodierungen, und in aller Regel Metall-Gliederarmbänder. Technophile Überinstrumentierungen – ein Techno-Barock, der von Mobiltelefonen über Kameras bis zu Stereoanlagen, CD-Playern und Notebooks digitalisierte Elektronikgeräte erfaßt hat – sind Meiers Sache nicht. Er spielt die auch bei seinen Armbanduhren durchaus avancierte Technik nicht in der visuellen Oberfläche aus: So sind die zahllosen Zifferblätter durchgehend von solider Dignität, die Lederarmbänder von einer ebensolchen gelassenen Eleganz gekennzeichnet. Wie schon am vielleicht folgenreichsten der Schweizer Entwerfer Max Bill sowie die schwedische Firma Jensen mit ihren Uhren gezeigt haben, dienen Klarheit und Reduktion mit ihrer minimalen Ästhetik der visuellen Eleganz am besten, ohne daß dies auf Kosten der Präzision geschehen müßte. Innerhalb einer solchen reduktiven Ästhetik bewegen sich auch die Chronometer dieses amerikanischen Architekten. Sie sind insofern jenen seines europäischen Kollegen Aldo Rossi sowie der »Movado«-Uhr des Museum of Modern Art in New York durchaus verwandt. Und eine der Meier-Uhren ist ebenso eine Hommage an ein Museum: an sein High Museum in Atlanta. Auch eine der beiden größeren Wanduhren Meiers für das nämliche Unternehmen ist ziffernlos, während die andere – offensichtlich in der formalen Tradition Max Bills – grazile Ziffern aufweist.

Der Kolbenfüller Meiers für die Acme Studios hat die klassische Vornehmheit europäischer Füller à la Montblanc oder Pelikan. Wiederum zeigt das durchsichtige Kolbenglas geometrisiertes Jugendstildekor; Füller und Füllerkappe haben kannelierte Ringe, und der Einsteckclip gehorcht der additiven Ästhetik mikroarchitektonischer Volumenseparierung. Mit wenigen besonderen Details also wird die ohnehin klassisch-elegante, handschmeichlerisch bauchige Zigarrenform des Füllers stilistisch positioniert.

Füller, Armbanduhren, Ringe – nimmt man noch Meiers Geldschein-Clips und seinen Schlüsselring hinzu, so wird deutlich, daß ihn neben Möbeln und Produkten für Tisch und Schreibtisch auch die Objekte mit unmittelbarem »Körperkontakt« interessieren: Auf Gürtel, Portemonnaies, Visitenkartenetuis, Feuerzeuge, Brillen, Manschettenknöpfe und Krawattennadeln Meiers darf man gespannt sein.

So richtet sich Meiers gestalterisches Interesse auf alle Felder der pragmatischen Ästhetik: »vom Löffel zur Stadt«, wie dies schon 1953 bei Ernesto Rogers hieß, in der Abstufung der den Menschen umgebenden »Häute« – persönliche Accessoires, Objekte für den gedeckten Tisch und den Schreibtisch, Mobiliar, private Häuser, öffentliche Gebäude, Gebäude-Ensembles. All dies aber sind Felder der »angewandten Kunst«, der Künste also, »die sich nützlich machen«. Wie aber steht es um die »freien« Künste?

Personal design

As of 1982, the Italian manufacturer Cleto Munari invited about 15 leading contemporary architects and designers to create a collection of precious jewelry pieces. Besides the Postmodernists Robert Venturi, Stanley Tigerman, Robert A. M. Stern, and Arata Isozaki, also the Neo-Modernists Ettore Scottsass and Alessandro Mendini, as well as Mario Bellini and Richard Meier were among the designers.

In 1985, Meier created two rings, which each consist of 18-karat gold adorned with black and white onyx. One of these rings is an almost classical, tripartited circle which is enlarged each time at the junctures. It uses for its »filling« an encircling row of black-and-white fields. This arrangement makes the design resemble the decorative element which we know from the façades of religious buildings of the Early-Renaissance period. The second ring is distinctly asymmetrical. It has an outcropping of onyx segments in form of a quarter circle of various dimensions and adjoining trapezoid shapes. All of these are positioned vertically to the finger and remind of the rough and protruding rustic stones used in Renaissance palaces. These »dancing« shapes rely on design details by Borromini and Alberti and they correspond to Meier's rational-labyrinthine interpenetrating spaces which he also uses in the language of his architecture. It is enriched through a reverence towards the 1920s and an allusion to earlier history. One might ask as well, if this black-and-white jewelry could be meant as a counter-reference to the jewelry of the Viennese Otto Wagner during the Art Nouveau period. If one does not read the design as a rhythmical sequence applied in the arrangement of piano keys, one could also interpret the work as a hint towards the logical arrangement of a chess board, here literally gone out-of-bounds.

Meier's wrist watches for the Markuse corporation are formally less extreme. His gentlemen's chronometers are characterized by the classical round face. On their rims which are devoid of numerals elegant hour- and minute hands dominate the appearance as well as Meier's own signature. Here, time is only measured in approximation, and the test of exactness of the day, as we use it in athletic competitions is here repudiated. In the words of Arnold Gehlen one might say: »This concerns ... disgust against a world, which bothers us with hundredths of seconds, with catastrophes in never-never land, with projections and a bombardement of demands, advice, and warnings. Each area of employment or profession ... is criticised, and robots stagger around on the moon.«[16]

Analogue gentlemen's watches likes these are »classical« in a certain way and by their nature less subject to the changes of fashions of the time than those of, maybe, their pendant counterparts for ladies, they also contradict the technically supercharged chronometers of astronauts, aquanauts, and airplane pilots, which preferably sport 15 to 20 additional functions. Such »engineer watches« frequently have extra outer rings around the face which can be manoeuvered and which serve as a compass or provide nautical codes. The wrist bands are normally made of steel links. This represents a technophile over-instrumentalization, a techno-Baroque which has taken hold with many digitalized electronic gadgets ranging from mobile telephones and cameras to stereo units, from CD-players to notebooks. They are not Meier's favorites. While his wristwatches certainly incorporate an advanced technology, he does not portray this on their surface. His watch faces throughout show great visual dignity and his leather watch bands are of an equally solid elegance. The Swiss designer Max Bill has probably applied this same attitude very sucessfully, similarly to the Swedish firm of Jensen. Their chronometers have proved that clarity, reduction of design, and a Minimalist elegance serve the visual elegance best. This effect does not have to be achieved at the cost of the product's precision. The chronometers of the American designer exist in the same area of Minimalist estheticism. In so far they are also related in the same manner to the watch of his European colleague Aldo Rossi and to the »Movado« chronometer of the New York Museum of Modern Art. One of Meier's watches equally pays homage to one of his museums, the High Museum in Atlanta. One of Meier's larger wall clocks for the same edifice is without numerals, while the other clock, obviously following the formal tradition of Max Bill, is graced by small number digits.

Meier's flask fountain pen for the Acme Studios has the classical dignity of European fountain pens such as Montblanc or Pelikan. Once again, the translucent piston glass shows the geometrical decor of the Art Nouveau. The pen and its closure cap show channeled rings, and the attachment clasp follows the additive esthetics of a micro-architectural separation of volumes. Thus, the fountain pen is by itself classically elegant with its touch-enticing, rounded cigar shape. It uses few special details, but declares a particular stylistic position.

The fountain pens, wrist chronometers, and rings, to which one might add Meier's money-clip and key ring, state clarily that Meier shows a personal interest in related areas. In addition to furnishings and implements for the dining and writing table, he is creatively involved with objects which have an immediate physical connection with the human body. One might anticipate from him further designs such as for belts, wallets, cases for private and business cards, cigarette lighters, eye glasses, cufflinks, or tie pins.

Indeed, Meier's interest as a designer extends across each and every field of pragmatical esthetics just like Ernesto Rogers stated in 1953 with the phrase »from the spoon to the city«. The idea distinguished the various layers or »skins« which surround us as human beings – beginning with personal accessories and continuing to the objects for the dining table and the writing table and further afield to furnishings, private residences, public buildings, and building-ensembles. All of these areas are fields of the »applied arts« which means that here »the arts (are) put to use«. But what might this means for the »liberal« arts?

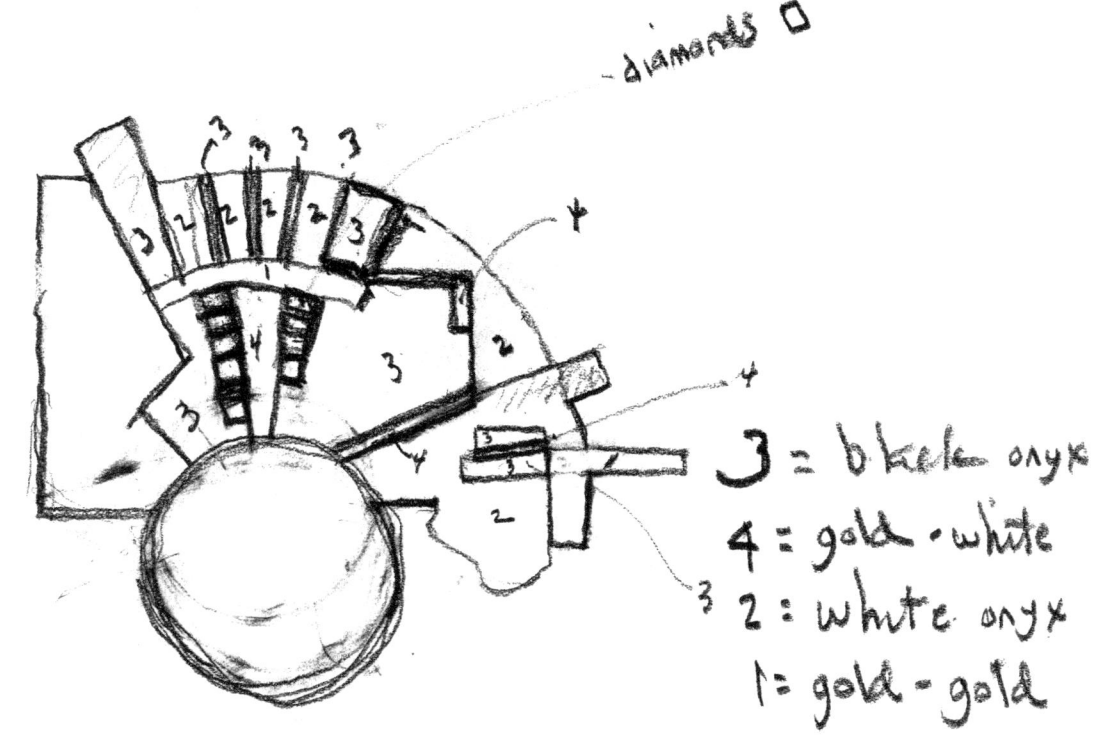

3 = black onyx
4 = gold - white
2 = white onyx
1 = gold - gold

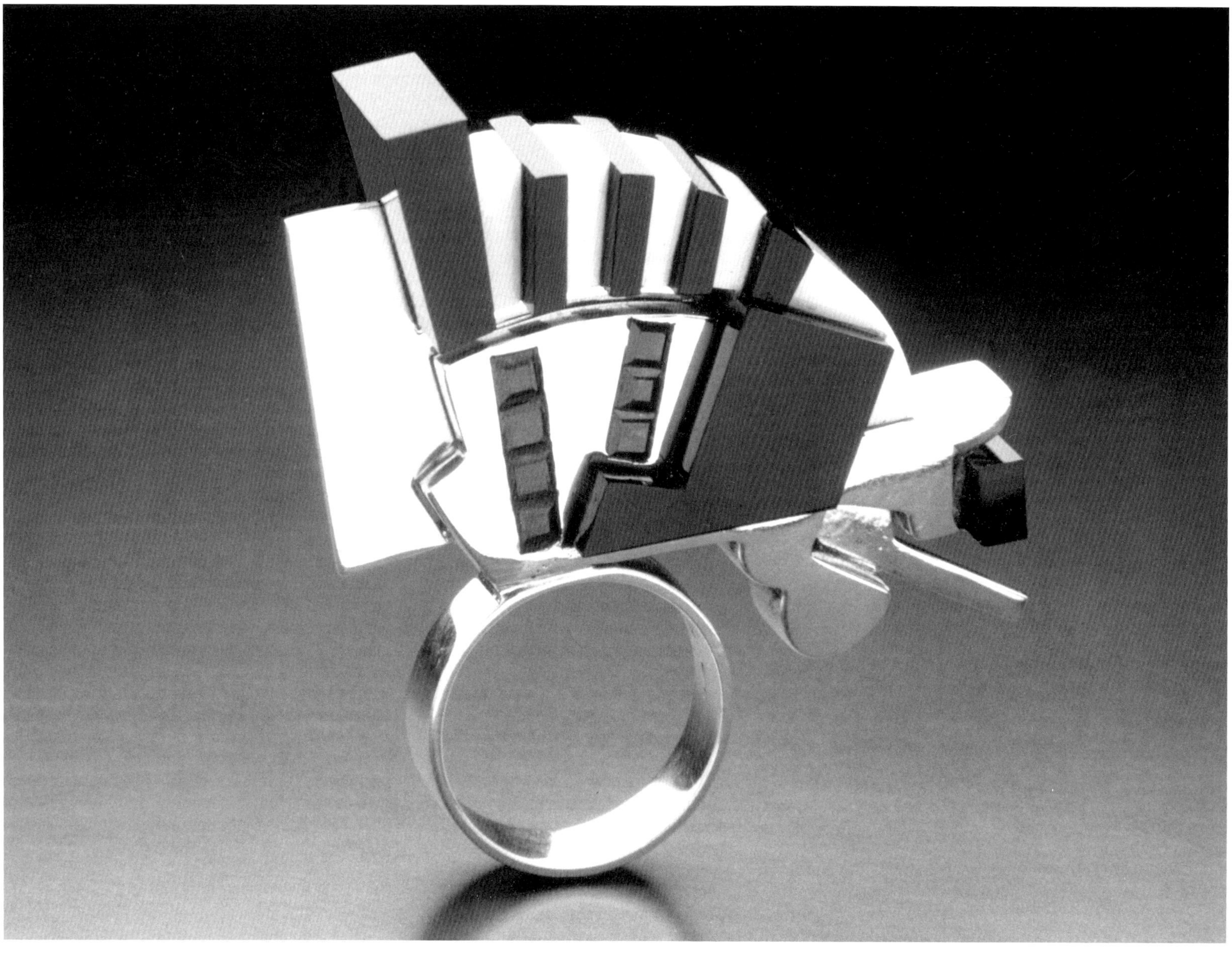

diamonds ▫

1, 2. Ring, 1985; Cleto Munari, Vicenza, Italien.
3. Ring, 1985; Cleto Munari, Vicenza, Italien.

1, 2. Ring, 1985; Cleto Munari, Vicenza, Italy.
3. Ring, 1985; Cleto Munari, Vicenza, Italy.

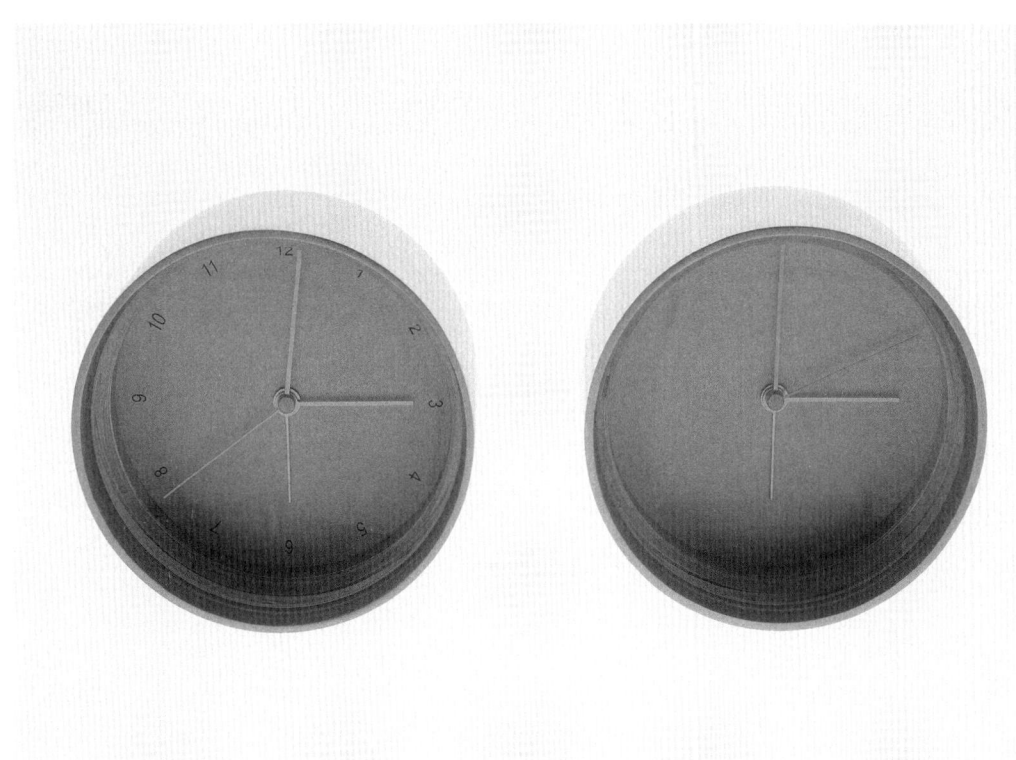

4. Wanduhren mit und ohne Ziffern, 2000; Jack Markuse Projects (The Markuse Corporation), Billerica, USA.
5. Armbanduhr »Montre« mit grauem Zifferblatt, schwarzem Band und Signatur; 1996, Armbanduhr »Montre« mit weißem Zifferblatt und weißem Band, 1996, Armbanduhr »High Museum« mit weißem Zifferblatt und Stahlband, 1998, sowie Armbanduhr »Montre« mit grauem Zifferblatt und Lederband, 1996; Jack Markuse Projects (The Markuse Corporation), Billerica, USA.
6. Füllfederhalter (Prototyp), 2002, Acme Studios, Kula, Maui, Hawaii.

4. Sleeper clocks with and without numbers, 2000; Jack Markuse Projects (The Markuse Corporation), Billerica, USA.
5. »Montre« watch with grey face, signature and black band, 1996, »Montre« watch with white face and white band, 1996, »High Museum« watch with white face and steel band, 1998, and »Montre« watch with grey face and black leather band, 1996; Jack Markuse Projects (The Markuse Corporation), Billerica, USA.
6. Fountain pen (prototype), 2002; Acme Studios, Kula, Maui, Hawaii.

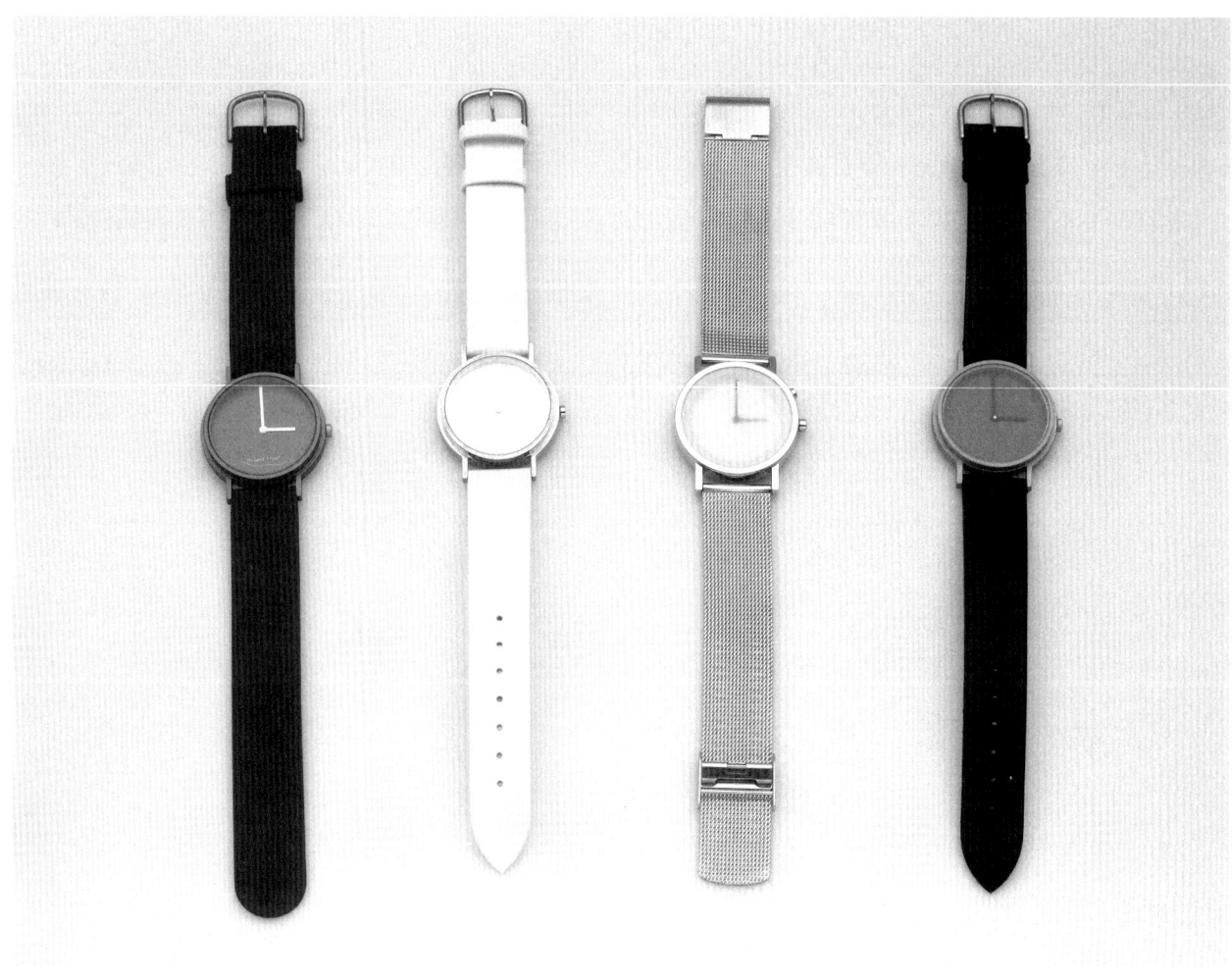

Collagen und Skulpturen

Es mag überraschend sein, von einem den pragmatischen Disziplinen wie Architektur und Design hauptberuflich verpflichteten Entwerfer auch freie künstlerische Arbeiten zu sehen. Und doch hat auch dies Tradition. So ist etwa das künstlerische Werk Le Corbusiers ebenso bedeutend wie seine Architektur oder sein Mobiliar. Das gleiche gilt für Peter Behrens, Josef Hoffmann, Koloman Moser, Otto Wagner oder Charles Rennie Mackintosh.

Die verschiedenen Serien von Collagen, die Richard Meier seit 1987 in immer gleichem Format von 27 x 27 cm gefertigt hat, sind auf einer strukturellen Ebene ebenso mit seiner Architektur dialektisch verbunden wie Le Corbusiers »Murals« mit seinen Nachkriegsbauten, etwa der Kapelle in Ronchamp. Doch während jener dem anthropomorph abstrahierenden Kubismus im Bauen und Malen verpflichtet blieb – und damit eine gute Prise Picasso und Juan Gris verarbeitet hat –, konzentriert sich Meier in seinen Collagen auf die Neuinterpretation konstruktivistischer Gedanken. Dabei bleiben seine Form- und Typographie-Kompositionen, die sich in Material, Farbe und Duktus etwa auf El Lissitzky, Tatlin, Malewitsch oder Rodtschenko berufen, intransigent gegenüber jedweder in sich geschlossenen Gegenständlichkeit. Fetzen der Realität – Gedrucktes, Typographisches, Plakatfragmente – entfalten im streng komponiertem Bildraum der Meierschen Quadratformate eine kompositorische Unruhe. Sie verweisen jeweils auf abwesende Inhalte, ohne diese konkret und plakativ abzubilden. Und eben dieser Verweischarakter kennzeichnet auch die raffinierten, ja manierierten Raumdispositionen, die überraschenden Durchdringungen von angeschnittenen Volumen, freien Raumscheiben, sich verjüngenden »Points de vue«, Rampen und verschachtelten Wahrnehmungsachsen der Meierschen Architekturen. Die Collagen gehorchen einer seriellen Logik und brechen doch jeweils für sich aus ihr aus. Ordnung und Chaos, Serialität und Individualität, Harmonie und Disharmonie, aber auch: Tradition und Innovation. All diese Gegensatzpaare sind für Meier sich gegenseitig bedingende; ja die Definition des einen Begriffs ist nur möglich in der Anschauung und Anerkennung des anderen. Erst die, immer kontrollierte, Störung der Form bringt diese recht eigentlich zur Erscheinung. Daß Meiers Collagen auch der Pop-Art à la Fritz Köthe, Wolf Vostell oder Mimmo Rotella mit deren Ausriß-Ästhetik überlappender Reste von Billboard-Plakatierungen formal einiges verdanken, belegt ein weiteres Mal, daß für diesen Entwerfer Vergangenheit gelebte und zu verarbeitende Gegenwart ist – und vice versa. Es geht eben auch um gegenwärtige Großstadtwirklichkeit, um plakatartige Montagebildtypen, um optische Zusammenfassungen der reizintensiven Fassaden großstädtischer Umwelt, um die Spiegelung eines von Kauflust und Werbung geprägten Lebensraums – Einflüsse, denen ein heute agierender Entwerfer sich nicht entziehen kann und wohl auch nicht will. Und doch beziehen sich Meiers Kompositionen auch auf den frühen synthetischen Kubismus der Schriftfragment-Collagen eines Pablo Picasso oder Georges Braque, Juan Gris und Carlo Carrà zwischen 1910 und 1915 sowie auf die Mitte der 1930er Jahre entstandenen Collagen von Kurt Schwitters. Auch die Typo-Montagen des italienischen Futurismus von Filippo Tommaso Marinetti oder Gino Severini sowie die sowjetrussischen Schriftcollagen von Alexander Rodtschenko, die Mitte der 20er Jahre nur aus Textstreifen und Zeitungsausschnitten zusammengesetzt wurden, oder die um 1915 entstandenen, ebenfalls Schriftfetzen verarbeitenden Collagen von Kasimir Malewitsch oder Ivan Puni sowie jene von George Grosz und John Heartfield mögen Anregungen geliefert haben. Die Kritikerin und Künstlerin Lois Nesbitt bemerkte 1990 zu Meiers Collagen und ihrem Entstehungszusammenhang: »Die eigentliche Idee einer Technik, die auf vorgefundenen Materialien basiert, verändert die Sterilität und Künstlichkeit der geschmackvollen Aufmachungen in Kunsthandlungen, und bevorzugt eine direktere Verbindung zwischen Dingen, die uns umgeben und denen, die in unsere Kunst Eingang finden. Richard Meier sammelt diverse Papierfetzen auf seinen Reisen (einige Entwürfe sind direkt während interkontinentaler Flüge in Skizzenbüchern entstanden), benutzt Material der täglichen Post, der Zeitungen und Magazine.« Sie beschrieb auch sehr genau die Beziehung zwischen Meiers Architektur und dessen »freier« Kunst: »Der differenzierte Farbsinn des Architekten (der in seinen reinen weißen Gebäuden deutlich fehlt) für die Abstufungen pastellfarbener Töne oder die kontrastreiche konstruktivistische Farbpalette von rot, schwarz, grau und weiß verdankt sich der Sensibilität eines Malers. Lange Jahre einer tief verwurzelten architektonischen Methode finden sich in diesen Papierarbeiten wieder. Eine sich wiederholende Anordnung – fließende diagonale Winkel, die den Rahmen fast füllen – erinnern an Meiers zahlreiche Architekturpläne, die auf ›Winkelverschiebungen‹ aufbauen und sich jeweils auf die Begrenzungen des Grundstücks beziehen. Frei geformte Kurven ausgerissener Papiere kontrastieren zu rechtwinkligen Elementen, die die an Corbusier orientierten Rundungen bestimmter Gebäude von Meier vorschlagen; wenn diese Kurven als unterbrochene Parallelen angelegt sind, gemahnen sie auch an die Konturen von Lageplänen. Überraschend gleichen bestimmte Buchstabenfragmente oder photographische Bilder ›zufälligen Ereignissen‹, oder nicht erzählerische Episoden unterstreichen bestimmte Elemente Meierscher Innenräume. Überlagerungen paralleler Raster oder orthogonaler Elemente rekapitulieren seine charakteristischen sektionalen Überlagerungen und komplizierten Muster von Fensteranordnungen.«[17]

Und schließlich gibt es jene schweren, massiven Metallskulpturen Richard Meiers, die jeweils etwa einen halben bis einen Kubikmeter einnehmen. Sie sind Hinweise nicht nur auf das Suchen, sondern auch auf die Überzeugung von subkutanen Energielinien, die das Entwerfen als Profession generell bestimmen. Dabei war die auslösende Erfahrung für Meier ein Besuch im Atelier seines Freundes Frank Stella: »Meiers Ausflug in die Geschichte der ›found-object‹-Skulpturen beruht angemessenerweise auf einem Zufall. Vor mehreren Jahren lud ihn sein Freund, der Künstler Frank Stella ein, die Tallix Foundry in der Peripherie New Yorks zu besuchen, in der Stella an großformatigen Skulpturen aus rostfrei-

1. Kasimir Malewitsch, *Stilleben mit Mona Lisa*, 1913.
2. El Lissitzky, Titelseite des Buches *Les Ismes de l'art* von El Lissitzky und Hans Arp, 1925.
3. Mimmo Rotella, *Avviso*, 1960.
4. Wolf Vostell, *Coca Cola*, 1961.

1. Kazimir Malevich, *Still Life with Mona Lisa*, 1913.
2. El Lissitzky, title page of the book *Les Ismes de l'art* by El Lissitzky and Hans Arp, 1925.
3. Mimmo Rotella, *Avviso*, 1960.
4. Wolf Vostell, *Coca Cola*, 1961.

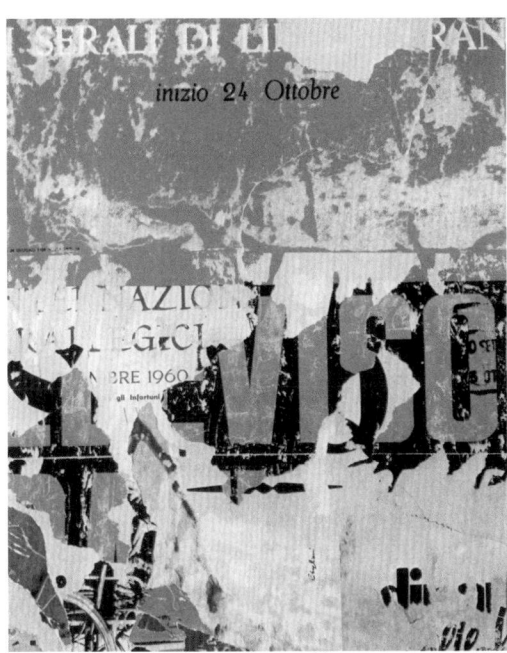

Collages and sculptures

It might surprise that there exist also free artistic creations from a designer whose main occupation lies in the field of the pragmatic disciplines of architecture and design. And yet, this phenomenon has its own traditions. For instance, the artistic work of Le Corbusier is equally as important as his architectural creations or his furniture pieces. One can say the same about Peter Behrens, Josef Hoffmann, Koloman Moser, Otto Wagner, or Charles Rennie Mackintosh.

The varied series of collages produced by Meier since 1987 and in the same 27 by 27 cm format are structurally and dialectically equally connected with his architecture as the »Murals« of Le Corbusier are connected with his post-War buildings such as the chapel at Ronchamp. But while the latter remained obliged to an antropomorphous and abstracting Cubism, which incorporated a good bit of Picasso and Juan Gris, Meier's collages take a concentrated aim at a new interpretation of Constructivist ideas. At the same time, his formal and typographical compositions which are somehow obliged in material, color, and characteristic lines to El Lissitzky, Tatlin, Malevich, or Rodtchenko, remain intransigent towards any self-contained physical objectivity. Pieces of everyday reality, i. e. prints, typographical materials, or poster fragments, together develop an artistic and compositional restlessness in Meier's strictly composed spatial images of his quadratic forms. Each time, they point towards some absent contents, but without portraying these concretely and in placard form. And this particular characteristic marks as well the ingenious and almost manieristic spatial distributions, the unexpected penetrations of volume segments, of independent spatial disks, of narrowing »points de vue«, ramps and encapsulated visual axes of Meier's architectural work. The collages follow a serial logic, but indivually they still free themselves from it: order and chaos, serial construction and indivual creation, harmony and disharmony, but also tradition and innovation. For Meier, these contrasting pairs complement each other; defining the one side, becomes possible only by understanding and accepting the other. Only by disturbing the form, which is always a controlled process, the true essence of it can ermerge. It is a fact that Meier's collages are formally indebted to Pop Art collages à la Fritz Köthe, Wolf Vostell or Mimmo Rotella with their tear-out estheticism of overlapping design pieces on bill board placards. This underlines once again that for this designer the past represents the living present in need to be creatively reshaped – or vice versa. But Meier is at the same time interested in the present-day reality of the big cities, in placard-like types of image collages. He works with optical concentration of sensually attractive fassades of the big city environment, devoting his energy to reflect his creativity in an area of day-to-day reality which us shaped by the desire to buy and the need to advertise. All these of life provide influences from which the creating designer of our day is unable to distance himself and, maybe, does not even wish to escape. And yet, Meier's compositions refer as well to the early, synthetical Cubism of the collages constructed of print fragments during the years of 1910 and 1915, works like those by Pablo Picasso or Georges Braque, of Juan Gris and Carlo Carra. Meier's own collages finally also remind of those by Kurt Schwitters created during the 1930's. Even the typo-montages of the Italian Futurism of Filippo Tommaso Marinetti or Gino Severini or the Soviet-Russian text collages of Alexander Rodtchenko, which during the middle of the 1920s only consisted of text pieces and newpaper clippings, might have provided a stimulus for Meier's own creations. The same indebtedness might be true with regard to the collages of Kazimir Malevich or Ivan Puni put together around 1915 from text fragments or to those by George Grosz and John Heartfield. In 1990, the art critic and artist Lois Nesbitt remarked about Meier's collages and about the background of their development: »The very idea of technique based on found materials challenged the sterility and artificiality of the neat arrays in art supply stores, favoring a more direct link between what we live with and what goes into our art. Richard Meier gathers his scraps of paper while traveling (some compositions are even executed in notebooks during intercontinental flights), out of the daily mail, from newspapers and magazines.« She also described precisely Meier's connection between architecture and his »liberal« artistic work as follows: »The architect's strong color sense (conspicuously absent in the pristine white buildings) for gradations of pastels or the high-contrast Constructivist palette of red, black, grey, and white derives from a painter's sensibility. But years of a now ingrained architectural method inflect these sketches in paper. A current configuration – the floating diagonal rectangle almost filling the frame – recalls Meier's many plans based on ›grid shifts‹ in relation to the edges of the site. The free-form curves of torn paper contrasting rectilinear elements suggest the Corbusian bulges of certain Meier buildings; when layered in loose parallels they also suggest the contour lines of site plans. Sudden, partial appearances of lettering or photographic images resemble the ›incidents‹ or non-narrative ›episodes‹ punctuating passages through Meier's interiors. Overlays of parallel grids or orthogonal elements echo his characteristic sectional layering and elaborate fenestration patterns.«[17]

And finally, there are those heavy, massive metal sculptures of Meier's, each of them filling approximately one-half to a full cubic meter of space. They give hints about his searching and about the persuasion of subcutaneous lines of energy which generally determine the profession of the designer. In this respect, for Meier the determining experience resulted from a visit in the atelier of his friend Frank Stella. »Meier's foray into found-object sculpture began, appropriately, by chance. Several years ago, Meier's long-time friend Frank Stella invited him to visit the Tallix Foundry in upstate New York, where Stella was working on large-scale works in cast stainless steel. While waiting for Stella to finish working, Meier busied himself in a corner, assembling wax elements and refuse into complex compositions. Eight hours later, when Stella had packed up to leave, Meier wanted to stay on. Thus began a passion that would consume his spare days and hours for the next three years, resulting in dozens

em Gußstahl arbeitete. Während Meier darauf wartete, daß Stella seine Arbeit zu Ende führte, schlenderte er in eine Ecke und beschäftigte sich damit, Reste aus Wachs zu komplexen Kompositionen zusammenzubauen. Nach acht Stunden, als Stella endlich aufhörte zu arbeiten, wollte Meier immer noch weiterbauen. So begann eine Leidenschaft, die seine freien Tage und Stunden mit dem Ergebnis Dutzender von Skulpturen die nächsten drei Jahre ausfüllen sollte.

Bald schon erweiterte Meier die ›gefundenen‹ Elemente für seine Skulpturen um Bruchstücke von Architekturmodellen, die sein Modellbau-Atelier in Los Angeles gesammelt hatte. Er verbindet diese Bruchstücke mit den ›gefundenen‹ Elementen mit Draht oder Fäden und taucht dann diesen Verbund in Wachs. Dies dient dazu, eine Negativform aus Keramik zu erhalten, die dann dazu dient, die Stücke in rostfreiem Stahl abzugießen. Insofern benutzt Meier die Überreste eigener Architekturentwürfe, manchmal kombiniert mit zusätzlich gefundenen Teilen, um diese Skulpturen zu kreieren. Für ihn bedeutet diese Art von künstlerischem Kannibalismus eine Möglichkeit, den abgelegten Modellen neues Leben einzuhauchen: Recycling als Wiederbelebung. Diese Methode verweist insofern auch auf eine poetische Einstellung. Meier nennt Teile alter Modelle, etwa die Rotunde des Getty Museums, die in verschiedenen Skulpturen auftaucht, ›Ruinen‹.«[18]

Dabei verweisen die Namen dieser Skulpturen – Ortsnamen süddeutscher Kleinstädte allesamt – nicht nur wie die Collagen auf Meiers Reiseerfahrungen, sondern auch auf seine, nur auf den ersten Blick überraschende, Begeisterung für die fließenden Räume des süddeutschen barocken Kirchenbaus. Dynamik, Richtungsgegensätze, vorausberechnete Licht- und Schattenwirkungen, das Integrieren von Einzelelementen in ein Gesamtkunstwerk, die Durchbrechung architektonischer Strukturen sind wesentlich für die barocke Architektur – und ebenso für die Bauten von Meier.

In ihren Gitterraum-Durchdringungen sind diese Skulpturen natürlich auch Hinweise auf Meiers architektonische Entwurfsmethode des »shifting of grids«, ebenso aber auch auf seine Faszination gegenüber »zweckfreien« räumlichen Kreationen in der Gattung Skulptur. Die weitaus spielerischer aufgefaßten kinetischen Skulpturen Jean Tinguelys kommen einem in den Sinn: nun aber ohne Bewegung, wie »eingefroren«. Beide aber verbindet der ästhetische Impuls, aus Resten, aus Abfall, vor allem aus Materialien, die noch der ersten industriellen Epoche angehören, »abstrakte« Erinnerungen zu destillieren. Insofern sind Meiers Skulpturen auch ein Hinweis auf die »heroische Zeit« der amerikanischen Eisen- und Stahlskelette, die Generationen von Hochhäusern erst ermöglichen. Aber diese Skelette haben keine geometrische »Ratio« mehr, sie sind ihrer »Utilität« und jedwedem Pragmatismus enthoben, Signets eines zweckfreien Spiels mit den ästhetischen Metamorphosemöglichkeiten der Material- und Dingwelt. Aber im Gegensatz zu Tinguelys Skulpturen oder auch jenen von John Chamberlain oder Louise Nevelson, von deren Objet-trouvé-Produkten einmal gesagt wurde, sie »sensibilisieren das profane Material auf die Magie der Zukunft hin«, sind Meiers Plastiken eben auch dreidimensionale Kalligraphien architektonischer Diskurse mit dem Signum vergangener, vergessener und abgetaner Produktionsprozesse. Sie sind, wie ein Eisenwalzwerker des 19. Jahrhundert wohl sagen würde, »ausgeglüht«: Mehr noch: Sie sind hybride Geschöpfe sowohl unseres wie eines längst untergegangenes Zeitalters.

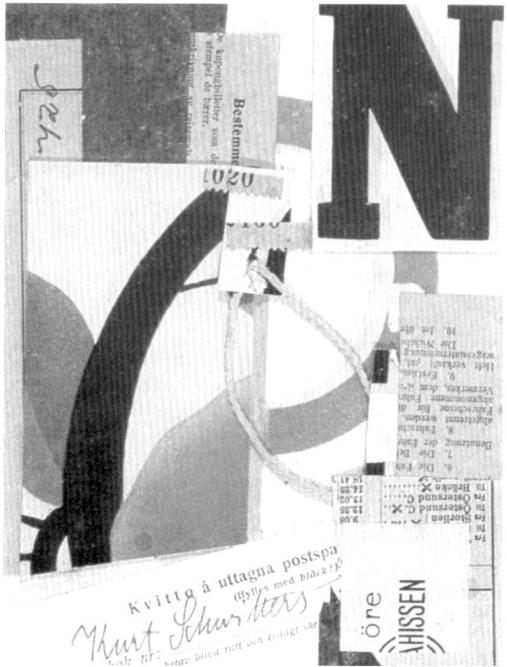

Diese abstrakten, wie durch Flammen gegangenen Raumgitter-Plastiken wirken wie miniaturisierte ausgeglühte Skelette statischer Perfektion. Ihnen ist das »Memento mori« als ästhetisches Programm eingeschrieben. Und doch entfalten sie eine fast zynische Kraft von Authentizität. Wem kämen jetzt nicht die Bilder von den skelettierten Tragwerksresten des World Trade Centers in den Sinn, die eine ikonographische Kraft jenseits der individuellen und kollektiven Trauer entwickelten? Meiers Skulpturen wirken wie ein Vorgriff auf solche apokalyptischen Ereignisse. So wie Brancusi das Menschenbild verzerrt, gedehnt, ja auch skelettiert hat, um das »Humanum« zu betonen, um Befindlichkeiten dieses Mensch-Seins herauszuarbeiten, so »entkleidet« Richard Meier in seinen Skulpturen den architektonischen Diskurs der Volumen, Fassaden und Räume, um ihre statischen und energetischen Charaktere sichtbar zu machen. Dies ist nicht wenig, das ist im Gegenteil viel für einen, wenn auch artifiziellen Pragmatiker, dessen architektonischem und produktkulturellem Werk Dignität, Solidität und der Glaube an die konstruktive Machbarkeit, mithin Beherrschbarkeit der Welt eingeschrieben scheinen. Es ist genau dieses »Shifting« zwischen rationalen Bezugsgrößen und emotionalen Obsessionen, welches den ästhetischen und intellektuellen Horizont dieses Entwerfers auszeichnet und ihn changieren und vibrieren läßt. Wie Guillaume Apollinaire sagte: »Der Weise lacht nur mit Zittern.« Dieser Aussage würde Richard Meier wohl zustimmen.

5. Kurt Schwitters, ohne Titel, 1936/37.
6. George Grosz, John Heartfield, *Dada-merika*, 1919.
7. Georges Braque, *Glas, Karaffe und Journal*, 1913/14.
8. Pablo Picasso, *Flasche, Glas und Geige*, 1913. Ausschnitt.

5. Kurt Schwitters, no title, 1936/37.
6. George Grosz, John Heartfield, *Dada-merika*, 1919.
7. Georges Braque, *Glass, Decanter and Journal*, 1913/14.
8. Pablo Picasso, *Bottle, Glass and Violin*, 1913. Detail.

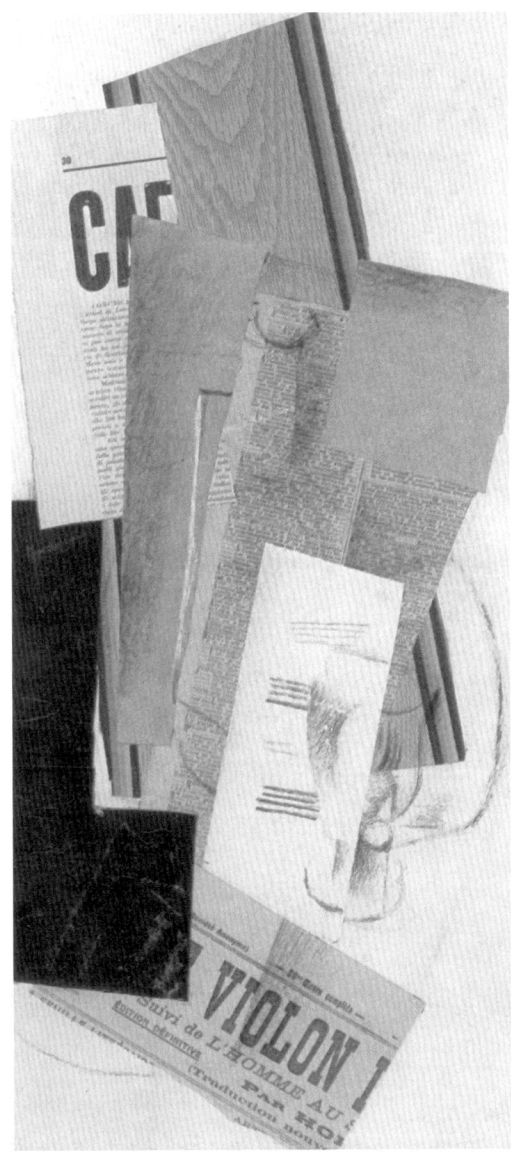

of sculptures. Meier soon expanded his found objects to include scraps of architectural models collected from his architectural model shop in Los Angeles. He binds these elements and items from the foundry together with string and then dips the whole bundle in wax. This is used to create a ceramic mould, which in turn provides the shell for casting the pieces in stainless steel. Meier thus uses the relics of his own design process, occasionally mixed with found objects, to create new works. He sees this kind of artistic cannibalism as a way of breathing new life into abandoned models: recycling as reanimation. The method also has a poetic slant. Meier calls old model parts, such as the rotunda from the Getty Museum that appears in several sculptures, ›ruins‹.«[18]

The names of Meier's sculptures – all of them names of small Southern-German towns – reflect not only, like the collages, his travel experiences, but also his enthusiasm for the floating spaces of the Baroque churches of Southern Germany, which is surprising only at a first sight. Dynamics, changing of directions, predefined effects of light and shadow, the integration of all details into a *Gesamtkunstwerk*, the fragmentation of architectural structures are essential for Baroque architecture – and also for Meier's buildings.

In their »grid-penetration« these sculptures are of course also hints towards Meier's architectural design method of the »shifting grids«, but also towards his fascination with »free-form« spatial creations in the area of sculpting. The much more playfully conceived kinetic sculptures by Jean Tinguely come to mind, but Meier's are without motion, like »frozen«. On the other hand, both are connected by the esthetical impulse, to distil »abstract« memories from remnants or refuse, especially from materials still belonging to the first Industrial Epoch. In this sense, Meier's sculptures also provide a reference towards the »heroic time« of the American iron-and-steel frame construction through whose existence alone the many generations of sky scrapers became possible. But Meier's skeletons have no remaining geometrical »ratio«; they have been relieved of any »utility« and pragmatism. They only remain signets of a functionally pointless game with the possibilities of esthetical metamorphosis within the world of materials and things. But contrary to the sculptures by Tinguely or those by John Chamberlain or Louise Nevelson the objet-trouvé production of which once has been said that they »sensitize profane materials towards the magic of the future«, Meier's sculptures are after all three-dimensional calligraphies within the architectural discourse and with an imprint of bye-gone and forgotten processes of production. These other works have »annealed«, as a 19th-century worker in an iron-rolling mill might have said. Beyond that, they are hybrid creations of our own as well as a bye-gone era.

These abstract spatial grids which seem to have passed through flames appear like miniaturized annealed skeletons of static perfection. The »memento mori« indwells them as their esthetical program. But they, nevertheless, contain an almost cynical power of authenticity. Who would at their sight not be reminded of the pictures of the remaining skeletal structure of the World Trade Center which developed an ikonographical power beyond all personal and collective mourning? Meier's sculptures create the impression of an anticipation of such apocalyptical events. Just like Brancusi contorts the human image, extending it, even renders it skeletal, in order to stress its »human element« or in order to underline the essence of what it means to be human, in the same sense Richard Meier »denudes« the architectural discourse of the volumes, outlines, and spatial reality of his sculptures, in order to make their structural and energetical properties visible. This is not a trifle, on the contrary, it is quite an accomplishment for someone, even as a creative pragmatic whose architectural and product-cultural work has an imprint of dignity, solidity, and a belief in the constructional feasibility, which means in the end in the possibility of controlling the world. It is exactly this »shifting« between the rational relativities and the emotional obsessions which characterizes the esthetical and intellectual horizons of this designer. These horizons develop a changeable and vibrating vitality. As Guillaume Apollinaire puts it: »The wise man only laughs with a certain trepedation.« Richard Meier would probably agree with this statement.

1. *S 12*, 3 August 1987.
2. *British Airways*, 8 August 1987.
3. *Berlin*, 11 August 1987.
4. *Russian/NHR, CN*, 16 August 1987.

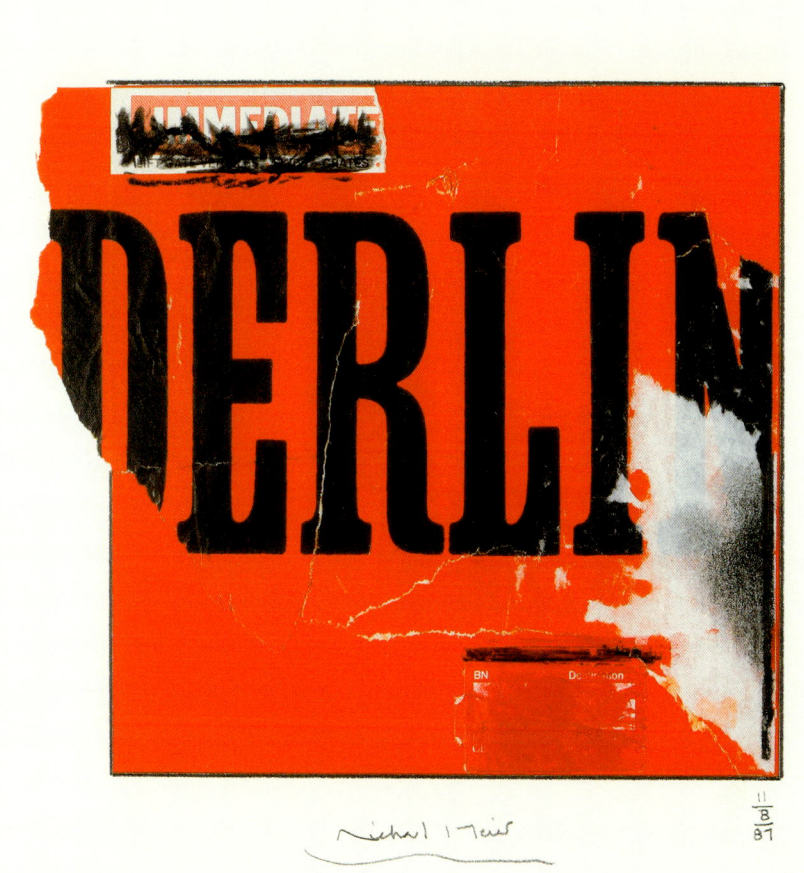

5. *Nella*, 27 August 1987.
6. *L'Art Decoratif M*, 11 September 1987.
7. *Interve*, 13 September 1987.
8. *Group Photo*, 16 September 1987.

9. *Aerolineas Grid*, 24 September 1987.
10. *Eintrittskarte*, 26 September 1987.

11. *Stuttgart Paquet*, 29 September 1987.
12. *Кресt*, 30 September 1987.
13. *16 – May 16*, 3 October 1987.

14. *Ana Meier, Hicksville, NY*, 8 October 1987.
15. *Row BB Orchest.*, 9 October 1987.
16. *A Building Direct*, 12 October 1987.

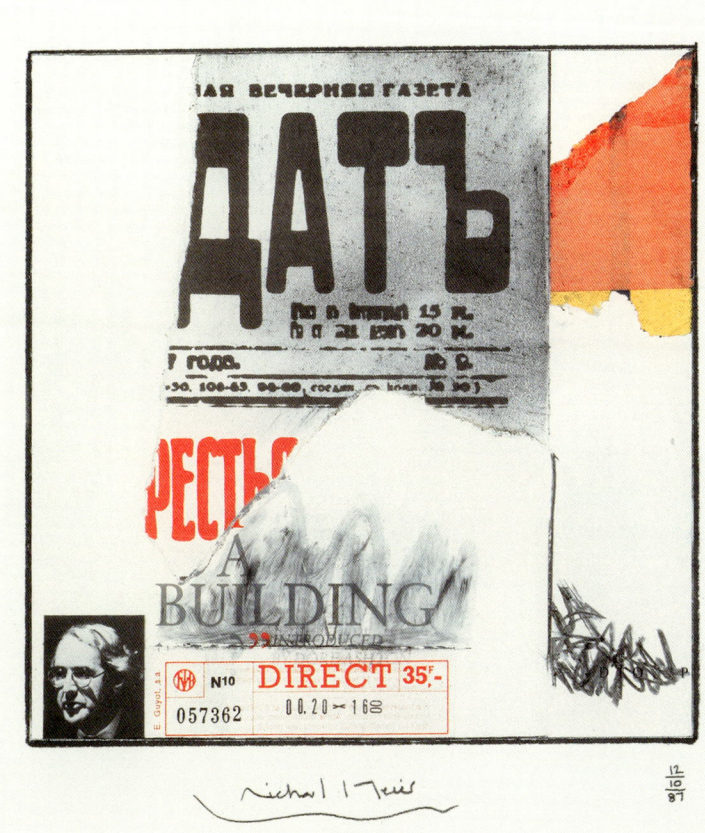

17. *Michael's Imprime*, 10 July 1990.
18. *Berlin Douane C-1*, 16 July 1990.
19. *Uguale Sull'o*, 18 July 1990.
20. *197 Gray*, 7 November 1996.

74

21. *Not Late*, 1 October 1998.
22. *1860 A Century of Style*, 31 November 1998.
23. *100 Drachmas*, 1 May 2002.

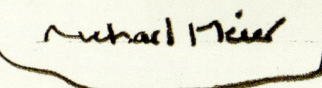

24. *Mockba*, 2 May 2002.
25. *Lane 3*, 3 May 2002.
26. *Mille Lire*, 4 May 2002.
27. *Pesos Argentinos*, 5 May 2002.

28. *Ottobeuren*, 1993.
29. *Neresheim*, 1993.

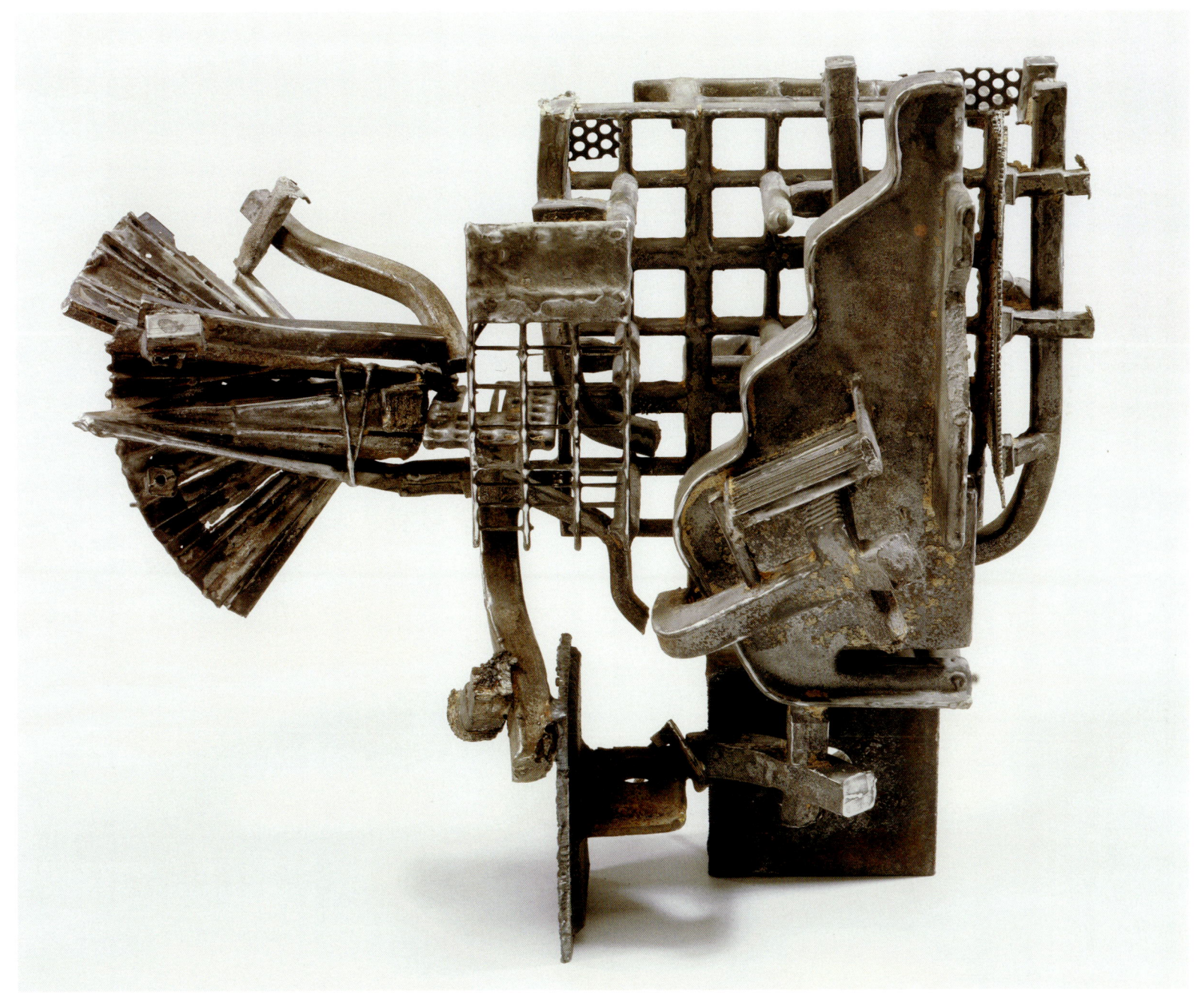

30. *Markdorf*, 1992.
31. *Bodman*, 1993.
32. *Saulgau*, 1994.
33. *Mimmenhausen*, 1994.

Das Museum für Angewandte Kunst in Frankfurt am Main

Die Geschichte des Museums beginnt mit einer gemeinnützigen Initiative Frankfurter Bürger, die sich 1877 zu seiner Gründung in einem Kunstgewerbe-Verein zusammenschlossen. 1921 wurde das Museum städtisch; dennoch lebte es immer auch vom Bürgersinn seiner Freunde und Mäzene. Nach der Zerstörung seines damaligen Domizils in der Neuen Mainzer Straße im Jahr 1944 konnten erst 1966 wieder Teile der Sammlung in der instandgesetzten Villa Metzler (erbaut 1803) am Schaumainkai gezeigt werden. In den schönen klassizistischen Räumen ließen sich aber nur fünf Prozent der Bestände ausstellen. 1979 schrieb deshalb das Hochbauamt der Stadt Frankfurt am Main einen internationalen Wettbewerb für einen Erweiterungsbau des Museums aus, an dem aus den USA Richard Meier sowie das Team Robert Venturi, John Rauch und Denise Scott-Brown, aus Österreich Hans Hollein und aus der Bundesrepublik das Team Johannes Peter Hölzinger und Hermann Goepfert, Heinz Mohl sowie die Büros Novotny/Mähner und Trint/Quast teilnahmen. Die Wettbewerbsjury erkannte im April 1980 dem Entwurf von Richard Meier einstimmig den 1. Preis zu. Baubeginn war im März 1982, und schon im August 1984 konnte das Gebäude der Museumsleitung zur Inneneinrichtung überlassen werden. Am 25. April 1985 wurde in Anwesenheit des damaligen Bundespräsidenten Richard von Weizsäcker der Bau seiner Bestimmung übergeben.

Vor allem war es sicherlich Meiers offene und gegliederte Raumplanung, die seinem Vorschlag gegenüber den anderen Projekten einen Vorteil verlieh. Denn es ging darum, die Villa Metzler in die größere geforderte Baumasse der neuen Gebäude zu integrieren und sie in die bestehende urbane Struktur des Schaumainkais auf dem zur Verfügung stehenden Parkgelände einzupassen. Meier respektierte die bestehende städtische Struktur und die Geschichte des Ortes, indem er sein Gebäude als eine hierarchisch modulierte Komposition von Kuben, Höfen und sich schneidenden Kreuzachsen auf die Villa Metzler bezog. Seine drei großen Neubaukuben, die mit einer Kantenlänge von 17,6 m die historischen Maße der Villa Metzler aufnehmen, legen sich wie eine offene miteinander verbundene L-Form um das historische Gebäude. Aber auch in der Harmonie der Außenfronten im Hinblick auf Größe, Maßstab und Rhythmus der Fenster orientierte sich Meier an dem vorhandenen Gebäude. Der L-förmige Komplex bildet einen internen Innenhof sowie sich schneidende Gebäudeachsen aus, wobei der Hof Alt- und Neubau-Ensemble als Ganzes zentriert und die Achsen das rechtwinklige Raster des Schaumainkais mit seinem prinzipiellen System vertikaler Wege verbinden. Meiers gesamter Plan wird von dieser normativen Kreuzachse geteilt, die sich in Koordinaten bis in den Park hinein verlängert. Räumliche Spannung ergibt sich durch das verbindende Überlappen zweier verschobener Achsenkreuze, die um 3,5 Grad voneinander abweichen. Diese Abweichung definiert auch die Ausrichtung des Eingangsbereichs und der Eckpavillons und setzt sich im gesamten Plan und auf jeder Ausstellungsebene fort. Dadurch weist das fertiggestellte Gebäude unregelmäßige, d. h. nicht-parallele Verkehrsflächen in jedem Stockwerk auf. Die drei Eckpavillons, quadratisch in ihrem prinzipiellen Grundriß, haben eine viersäulige strukturelle Logik, die sich aus der Übereinstimmung zwischen dem Raster der Fensterstreben und den Verbindungen der modularen Fassadenelemente ergibt. Vom Eingangspavillon aus führt eine großzügig dimensionierte Fußgängerrampe, die nicht zufällig an die »Schiffsmetaphorik« der klassischen Moderne – etwa an das Haus Schminke von Hans Scharoun – erinnert, in alle Ausstellungsebenen. Zudem verbindet im ersten Geschoß eine verglaste Brücke den Neubau mit der historischen Villa Metzler. Der Architekturkritiker Joseph Rykwert hat Meiers Frankfurter Museum als durchgehend geometrisch geordnet charakterisiert und richtigerweise darauf hingewiesen, daß er damit dem Corbusierschen Ausgangspunkt seiner Arbeit am nächsten gekommen sei. Doch gibt es zweifellos gewisse figurative, dekorative und architektonische Elemente, die Meiers Bau von der Schlichtheit des Corbusierschen Funktionalismus abheben und ihm fast neobarocke räumliche Qualitäten verleihen. Zwar bewahrt er die durchgängig weiße Reinheit der Corbusierschen Anregung, überblendet sie jedoch mit einem fast wehmütigen Utopismus der Jahrhundertwende um 1900. Und so ist es mehr als bloßer Zufall, wenn in den Präsentationszeichnungen und Isometrien seines Wettbewerbsbeitrags das verputzte Foyer, die Vorhöfe und der Park mit Persönlichkeiten aus Otto Wagners Wien der Jahrhundertwende ausstaffiert sind. Kenneth Frampton hat darauf hingewiesen, daß dem Bau insgesamt auch in seiner Struktur und Verkleidung der Außenfassaden »ein Element liebenswürdigen bürgerlichen Anstands, ein Gefühl kultivierter Verführung, eine nicht greifbare Leichtigkeit« eigen sei, »die in den eröffneten Perspektiven der gerasterten Verglasung durchdringt und sich fließend in den Park und durch die Bäume fortsetzt und die schwermütige Weitläufigkeit einer anderen, kultivierteren Zeit heraufbeschwört«.[19] Und im Hinblick auf die entwurfsbestimmende Villa Metzler weist Norbert Huse auf ein weiteres Spezifikum dieses Museumsgebäudes hin: »Reminiszenzen an die Baukunst des 18. Jahrhunderts sind nicht zufällig, sondern gewollt, denn Meier interpretiert die Villa Metzler von 1803 nicht als ein Bau des Vor- oder Frühklassizismus, sondern als einen späten Abkömmling des deutschen Barock. So sah er für den Park ursprünglich beschnittene Hecken in geometrischer Anordnung vor.«[20] Und Huse weiter: »Ist der Bau einmal in das Assoziationsfeld ›Barock-Architektur‹ gerückt, dann gewinnt auch die Gestaltung des Zentrums neuen Sinn. Wo man im Barockpalast Corps de logis und Festsaal gefunden hätte, gibt es im Erdgeschoß eine Durchgangsstraße und im Piano nobile bis zum Boden reichende Fenster, die auch im Inneren an das Achsenkreuz der Wege erinnern. Das Zentrum des Bauwerks dient nicht der Repräsentation, sondern der Kommunikation. Für das Innere des Frankfurter Museums hat sich Meier erklärtermaßen an den Zielen orientiert, denen das Museum im Zeitalter der Aufklärung dienen sollte, und aus dieser Zeit, in der die festen Ordnungen des Barock wenn nicht aufgehoben, so doch in Frage gestellt wurden, stammt auch der Begriff

1, 2. Richard Meier, Fassadenstudien zur Villa Metzler und zum Neubau des Museums für Angewandte Kunst in Frankfurt, 1979/80.

1, 2. Richard Meier, façade studies of the Villa Metzler and the new building of the Museum for Applied Arts in Frankfurt, 1979/80.

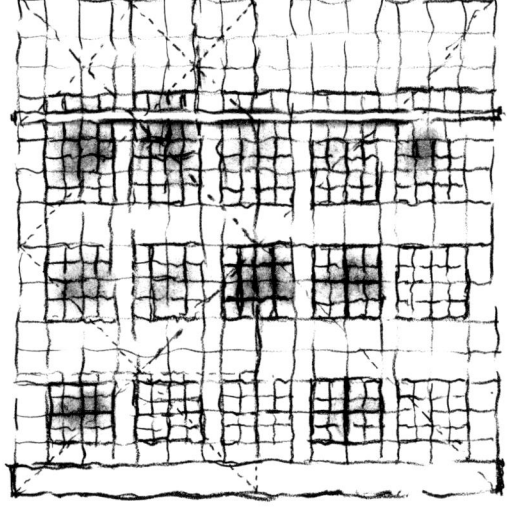

The Museum for Applied Arts in Frankfurt am Main

The history of the museum begins with the initiative of a number of Frankfurt citizens who in 1877 joined ranks to found a society for arts and crafts. In 1921, the museum was purchased by the City of Frankfurt. Nevertheless, it continued to be supported by its friends and benefactors in the city. After the destruction of its former home in the Mainzer Straße in 1944, it took until 1966 to reestablish parts of its collection in the renovated Villa Metzler (built in 1803) situated at the Schaumainkai on the banks of the river Main. Unfortunately, only an approximate five percent of the museum holdings could be exhibited in these beautiful Classicist rooms. Therefore, in 1979, the City of Frankfurt am Main launched an international competition to support the expansion of the museum. Among the participants were Richard Meier and the team Robert Venturi, John Rauch and Denise Scott-Brown from the USA, Hans Hollein from Austria, and the team Johannes Peter Hölzinger and Hermann Goepfert, Heinz Mohl, Novottny/Mähner, and Trint/Quast from the Federal Republic of Germany. The competition jury unanimously awarded the design of Richard Meier with the first prize in April 1980. The building construction began in March 1982, and as early as August of 1984, the building was ready to be handed over to the leadership of the museum in order to begin interior furnishing and decoration. On 25 April 1985 the building was opened to the public in the presence of the then President of the Federal Republic, Richard von Weizsäcker.

One may assume that it was due to Meier's open and well structured spatial planning which made his design suggestions more attractive. After all, the goal was to integrate the Villa Metzler into the required amplified volumes of new buildings and to integrate everything within the framework of the available parklands and the existing urban structure along the Schaumainkai. Meier considered this urban structure and the history of the place by relating his building design to the Villa Metzler in an all-encompassing hierarchically modulated composition of cubic structures, courtyards, and intersecting axes. The three large new building cubes whose sides of 17.6 m repeat the historical measures of the Villa Metzler, surround the historical edifice in an inter-connected open L-shape. But Meier also remained closely oriented towards the existing layout with regard to the harmony of the exterior walls, by size, by scale, and by the rhythmical intervals of the window arrangement. The L-shaped central complex of the new composition creates an internal courtyard and has intersecting structural axes, the courtyard surrounding the old and the new buildings as a central entity, while with its basic system of vertical pathways connecting the right-angled conceptual framework of the Schaumainkai. Meier's entire concept is divided by this normative cross-axis whose coordinates extend right into the park. The two overlapping and connecting shifted axes deviate one from the other by 3.5 degrees and create a spatial tension. The shift also defines the placement of the entrance and of the corner pavilions. It is continued throughout the entire layout of the museum complex and on each of its exhibition levels. This way, the completed building complex presents irregular, i. e. non-parallel areas of circulation on each of its levels. The three corner pavilions with their overall square base design, are logically structured by four-column arrangements which is a result of a correspondence between the window distribution and the connections with the modular elements of the façades. Beginning at the entrance pavilion, a pedestrian ramp of generous proportions leads towards all exhibitions areas. It is not by accident that this ramp reminds of the »ship metaphorics« of classical Modernism used, for instance at the Schminke House by Hans Scharoun. In addition, a glass-covered bridge connects the new building with the historical Villa Metzler on the first floor. The architectural critic Joseph Rykwert has characterized Meier's museum in Frankfurt as throughout geometrically arranged and has correctly emphasized that Meier here came closest to the initial beginnings of his work with Le Corbusier. And yet, there also exist without doubt certain figurative, decorative, and architectural elements which distinguish Meier's building design from the simplicity of Le Corbusier's functionalism and which lend it almost Neo-Baroque spatial qualities. While Meier retains the original white purity of color throughout the structure, a stimulus he had taken from Corbusier, he surrounds it with an almost utopian nostalgia as we know it from the turn of the century around 1900. And therefore, it is more than a mere accident when the drawings and isometric sketches of his design contributions for the competition – his plastered foyer, his atriums, and the park as well – are dressed up with characters from Otto Wagner's Vienna around the turn of the century. Kenneth Frampton has pointed out that also the remainder of the edifice in structure and facing of its outer façades represents »a sense of gentle bourgeois decorum to the work, a feeling of cultivated seductiveness, of a non-consumerist lightness, which in the published perspectives infiltrates the gridded glazing and the skylights and extends fluidly into the park, through the trees to recall the wistful spaciousness of another more leisured time.«[19] And with regard to the structure of the Villa Metzler which determined the design development for the entire architectural competition, Norbert Huse points out an additional and more specific detail of this museum structure: »Reminiscences of 18th-century architecture are not fortuitous but intentional, for Meier interprets the Villa Metzler, dating from 1803, not as a building of the Pre- or Early Classicism period but as a late descendant of German Baroque. Thus he originally envisaged for the park clipped hedges in geometrical arrangement.«[20] Huse continues: »Once the building has been associated with ›Baroque architecture‹, the design of the center takes on a new meaning. Where, in a Baroque palace, we would have found the corps de logis and the banqueting hall, here we find, on the ground floor, a thorough-fare, and, on the piano nobile, windows reaching down to the floor which, even from inside, remind us of the intersection of the path axes. The central portion of the building is dedicated not to representation but to communication. For the interior of the Frankfurt museum Meier avowedly adopted the

von Öffentlichkeit, der das Verhältnis von innen und außen bestimmt und zur Preisgabe des geschlossenen Blocks führt.«[21] Meier selbst hat dies präzisiert, indem er ausführt: »Im Erdgeschoß verbindet sich das Museum am engsten mit seiner Umgebung: Hier durchdringen sich Innen und Außen sowie die Öffentlichkeit der Stadt mit der Öffentlichkeit des Museums. Offene Passagen, welche die Fußwege des Parks mit dem Eingangshof verbinden, durchfluten das Geschoß mit Licht, Luft und Freiraum ... Die Offenheit des Geschosses gestattet Vorbeigehenden Einblicke ins Hausinnere, die anregen, das Gebäude zu betreten. Das Eingangsfoyer empfängt sie als eine offene, nach innen sich fortsetzende Erweiterung des Eingangshofes.«[22] An anderer Stelle spricht Meier von einer »Architektur reicher Collagen, komplexer Schichtungen und metamorphischer Bilder«.[23] Schließlich verallgemeinert er die Aussage über seine prinzipielle Entwurfsstrategie, wenn er sagt: »Der primäre Dialog aber bleibt der architektonische, in dem der Stuck und der Stein der Villa Metzler und die metallenen Paneele des Erweiterungsbaus viel über die Kultur und die Geschichte enthüllen, die ihr Nebeneinander hervorgebracht haben.«[24]

Bis heute ziehen die Komplexität und fast monadische Perfektion dieser Architektur Fachstudenten aus aller Welt an. Aber wenn es in den ersten Jahren der Nutzung des Neubaus primär darum ging, nun endlich den wenigstens größeren Teil der Museumsbestände öffentlich zeigen zu können, so wurde im Laufe der Zeit die Notwendigkeit dringender, auch die museologische Konzeption, die Programmatik der dargebotenen Inhalte mithin, komplexer und dialektischer zu fassen. Einen eher äußerlichen Anlaß dafür, dies auch in sensiblen innenarchitektonischen Aktualisierungen deutlich zu machen, bot das 15jährige Jubiläum der Einweihung des Neubaus im Juni 2000.

Das Museum als Institution – Ziele, Strategien, Programme

Zum Jubiläum des Neubaus wurde das Museum inhaltlich in seinen Angeboten, aber auch in seiner Innenarchitektur aktualisiert. Die vorhandenen, auf umfangreichen Sammlungsbeständen beruhenden permanenten Abteilungen für das Kunsthandwerk der klassischen europäischen Epochen vom Mittelalter über Renaissance, Barock und Klassizismus, Rokoko und Jugendstil bis zu herausragenden Leistungen des Kunsthandwerks im 20. Jahrhundert und den Abteilungen für fernöstliches Kunsthandwerk aus China, Japan und Korea sowie des Islam wurden ergänzt durch eine Abteilung für Design, also für industrielle Formgebung, sowie durch eine Forschungsabteilung »Digital Craft«, die Fragestellungen der digitalen, zeitgenössischen Welt und Umwelt untersucht und thematisiert. Die ausgestellten Sammlungsbestände des Museums wurden neu gruppiert und fokussiert unter Leitfragen, dominanten Dialektiken der jeweiligen Epochen oder Länder: Damit ist eine erzählerische, auch intellektuelle Dimension hinzugewonnen, die das Museum vorher nur punktuell charakterisierte. Viele Bestandsvitrinen wurden mit eigens neu entworfenen Sitzmöglichkeiten versehen, andere mit kindersicheren Leitern, um auch den kleinen Leuten Einblicke zu geben, die bisher den Erwachsenen vorbehalten waren. Ein solches Neuarrangement des Bestandes bedeutet immer auch seine Neubewertung, im Hinblick auf kontextuelle Signifikanz, kunsthistorische Einschätzung, kulturelle Anschlußfähigkeit an die Gegenwart, ästhetische Korrektiv- und Vorbildfunktion für unseren oft beklagenswert gestalt- und niveaulosen Alltag.[25]

Einige wenige schlaglichtartige Fragestellungen mögen die Richtung für die Neustrukturierung der Bestandsabteilungen verdeutlichen: So werden z. B. in der fernöstlichen Abteilung die Fragen von »Unikat und Serie« an 2000 Jahre altem Porzellan thematisiert oder »Ornament und Abstraktion« anhand von antiken Gefäßserien aufgerollt. In der Mittelalter-Abteilung werden u. a. »Minne – Begegnung von Mann und Frau«, in der Renaissance-Abteilung »Ornament und Mensch« thematisiert, beim Barock geht es um »Bewegung und Symmetrie« oder »Manufaktur contra Werkstatt«, im Klassizismus um »Bürgertum und Aufklärung«. Die Design-Abteilung stellt ebenfalls die Frage nach der zeitgenössischen Bedeutung einer Re-Ornamentalisierung im Entwerfen, beleuchtet emotionale Produkte und zeigt, daß die grassierende Semitransparenz von Kunststoffen einerseits die Veredelung des Banalen, andererseits die angebliche Durchschaubarkeit der Technik zum Thema hat. Man sieht, daß einer lediglich historiographischen Aufteilung der kunsthandwerklichen Spitzenstücke der diversen Epochen konzeptionell widersprochen wird: Was sind die »Leitfragen« einer Epoche, was hat sie gestalterisch und gesellschaftlich beschäftigt, was überhaupt ist ihr Diskurs, der uns auch heute noch animieren und anregen kann?

Kommunikation und Lernen

Museen für angewandte Kunst bieten üblicherweise praktische Kurse an: in Papierschöpfen, in klassischen Drucktechniken wie Radierung oder Lithographie, in dreidimensional bildnerischen Umsetzungen von Objekten der Sammlung. Das neu positionierte Museum für Angewandte Kunst in Frankfurt hat all dies beibehalten und doch ergänzt: z. B. um computergestützte Kurse, in denen Kinder und Jugendliche, aber auch Erwachsene, spielerisch-kreativ in die Techniken und Denkwelten der Digitalisierung eingeführt werden. Ebenso hat das Museum sein Veranstaltungsangebot intensiviert. Unter dem Label »mak.zusammen« aktualisiert eine frühabendliche tägliche Diskussionsreihe von Dienstag bis Samstag die vergangenen und unterschiedlichen Kulturen. Das »spek.takel« am Mittwoch bietet Führungen mit Wissenschaftlern und/oder Schauspielern. Der Donnerstag ist der Betrachtung und Bewertung von Objekten gewidmet: »con.versazione«, der Freitag setzt mit »sa.lon« auf inhaltlichen und intellektuellen Austausch. Und schließlich gibt es jeden ersten Samstag im Monat ein Programm zur Tisch- und Eßkultur mit Geschmacksschule und Menüpremiere: »happy.hour«. Hier werden Produkte aus den Museumssammlungen benutzt und mit damit in Zusammenhang stehenden Aktivitäten wie Weinproben und speziellen Abendessen verknüpft.

aims which museums where expected to serve in the age of Enlightenment, and from this period, in which the strict orders of Baroque art had not yet been swept away but were certainly being questioned, comes the concept of ›publicness‹, determining the relationship between interior and exterior, and leading to the abandonment of the closed block.«[21] Meier himself has precisely explained this idea when he states: »At the ground-floor level occurs the strongest interaction between the building and its surroundings, a filtering between inside and outside, between passersby and Museum visitors. Open passageways connect the Park footpaths with the plaza, allow light, air and space to penetrate ...The transparency of this level gives passersby views into the Museum, inducing them to enter; the Northwest Quadrant, the Entry Hall, is designed as an open, interior extension of the plaza.«[22] At another place, Meier speaks about an »architecture of rich collages, of complex layering, and of metamorphic pictures.«[23] Finally, he generalizes the explanation of his design strategy when he states: »But the primary dialogue remains the architectural one, in which the stucco and stone of the Villa Metzler and the metal panels of the extension beside it reveal much about the culture and history that have produced their juxtaposition.«[24]

Up to this day, the complexity and the almost monadic perfection of this architecture attracts students of the field from all across the world. But while the first few years after opening were spent in an attempt to finally display the largest possible amount of its holdings, it became increasingly necessary over the years to address the complex dialectic of the building's museology. An opportunity offered itself in June 2000, the 15th jubilee of the inauguration of the new building, when these ideas were realized in a sensitive remodeling of its interior architectural design.

The museum as an institution: its goals, strategies, and programs

On the occasion of the 15th anniversary of the opening of the new building, the museum's permanent collections as well as its internal architecture were remodeled. The existing exhibitions were complemented and expanded from the extensive permanent displays of European Arts and Crafts, stretching from the Middle Ages, through the Renaissance, Baroque and Classicism, the Rococo period and Art Nouveau up to the most important accomplishments of the 20th century. Moreover, the improvements also affected the existing collections of the arts and crafts of China, Japan, and Korea, as well as those of Islam, and for the first time, the museum had a new permanent exhibition of industrial design. It also included a permanent collection of difficult to preserve »digital craft« including websites, computer games, and digital artifacts. The permanent exhibitions of the museum were re-grouped and re-focussed. This process added a narrative as well as an intellectual dimension to the entire design concept which heretofore the museum had only offered in some of its segments. Seating arrangements were added to many of the showcases, other showcases were installed with child-safe ladder arrangements to allow children to see into adult-height showcases. Such a reshuffling of the basic elements of the museum necessarily meant a re-evaluation, both of its general significance, its art historical value, and its ability to adapt to contemporary circumstances. Moreover, the re-installation confirmed the museum's mission to provide an new example of active engagement in our often culturally impoverished daily lives.[25]

A few of the guiding principles may indicate the museum's new direction and exemplify the structural renewal of the various permanent exhibitions of the museum. For instance, the Far-Eastern collection highlights the questions of »individual pieces and serial production« using the example of the museum's outstanding collection of 2000-year-old porcelain. The section also treats the question of »ornament and abstraction« by comparing collections of antique containers. The exhibition of the applied arts of the Middles Ages, for instance, explores the theme of »minne: or the relationship between man and woman«; the Renaissance exhibition uses as its theme »ornament and man«; the exhibition of Baroque applied art is concerned with »movement and symmetry« or »manufacturing versus the workshop«; while the exhibition of Classicism looks at »the middle classes during the Age of Enlightenment«. The permanent exhibition of design concerns itself with contemporary questions about the meaning of re-ornamentation in the context of structural design, while it illustrates and explains some rather sensitive products. For instance, it shows that the semi-transparency of synthetic materials serves on one hand the refinement of banal functions and on the other hand serves the alleged transparency of all technology today. It is apparent that this concept contradicts the merely historiographical arrangement and display of great art and crafts pieces of the various periods. Instead the new concept explores the leading problems of the time such as »What are its structural and social concerns?« or »What are the issues that can still excite and animate us today?«

Communication and learning

Museums for Applied Art usually offer practical courses in fields such as paper-making, the classical printing techniques such as etching or lithography, or the study of objects in the collection as three-dimensional forms. The newly arranged Museum for Applied Art in Frankfurt has retained these practices and has expanded them further. For example, it has added computer-assisted courses in which both children and adults can be introduced in a playfully and creative way to the new techniques of digitalization. As a consequence, the museum has attracted a group of young adults especially for the purpose of testing computer games as one of the criteria for selecting them for the museum's growing collection of digital artifacts – so-called »Digital Craft«. The museum has also increased its offer of other events. Under the label »mak.zusammen«, an early-evening session of discussions from Tuesday through Friday probes past cultures as well

Auch in der Ansprache jüngerer Besucher geht das Museum neue Wege. Zusätzlich zu dem Projekt »Digital Craft«, welches Teenager und junge Erwachsene mit Ausstellungen wie »I love you: Computer, Viren, Hacker und Kultur«(2002) anspricht, gibt es einen Kinderführer, interaktive Ausstellungen und spezielle didaktische »Abteilungskoffer«, um Familien Anregungen bei der Entdeckung der Museumsschätze anzubieten. Mehr noch: eine spezielle Gruppe junger Studenten der Kunstgeschichte – mit dem Namen »mak.crew« – steht für Informationen, Ratschläge und spontane Führungen zur Verfügung.

Café-Restaurant und Museumsshop

Es gehört heute zu den unbestrittenen Sekundärangeboten eines internationalen Museums, qualitätvolle Angebote für Shopping und Gastronomie bereitzustellen. Als das Museum für Angewandte Kunst gebaut wurde, war von Anfang an ein Restaurant mit einer Kapazität von etwa 200 Sitzplätzen innen und außen integrierter Bestandteil der Planung. Das Café wurde von Richard Meier in modernistisch bereinigtem Stil eines Wiener Cafés möbliert. Es gab eine Kuchen- und eine Salattheke, aber weder eine Bar noch eine Lounge-Ecke für die entspannte Lektüre internationaler Gazetten bei einem Longdrink zur »happy hour«. Dies hat das Museum in der Phase seiner Neupositionierung geändert. Heute ist das Restaurant nicht einfach ein Restaurant, sondern ein Ort, an dem angewandte Künste anders und sinnlicher als bloß in Vitrinen erfahren werden können. Die Schönheit eines Kristallglases kommt erst mit einem exquisiten Wein zur Geltung, und eine japanische Lackschale entfaltet ihren Zauber besonders dann, wenn knisternder Reis oder Sushi in ihr angeboten wird. Darüber hinaus werden exquisite Weinproben in historischen Gläsern ebenso wie spezielle Dinner auf Porzellan von renommierten Designern angeboten. Insofern sind Ausstattung und Speisen mit den Museumssammlungen verbunden. Das Restaurant wird so zur »Bühne«, auf der die angewandte Kunst »aufgeführt« wird.

Das Café-Restaurant wurde nach Planungen des Frankfurter Architekten und Designers Uwe Fischer vollständig umgebaut, ein Raum hinzugewonnen, eine Bar installiert und der verfügbare Raum in Restaurant, Bar und Bistro differenziert. Die Öffnungszeit, ehemals limitiert bis 19 Uhr, ist ausgeweitet bis 24 Uhr oder später und unterstützt damit das Museum mit seiner bis 20 Uhr erweiterten Öffnungszeit. Der Raum selbst, ehemals mit Teppichboden und Wiener Caféhausstühlen bestückt, wurde entkernt und mit Eichenparkett, neuen, leichten Stühlen des Belgiers Gert van Severen und elegantem Lederequipment in hellen Tönen aktualisiert. Die neu installierten innenarchitektonischen Elemente haben den Raum architektonisch aktualisiert; ein Konzept, welches manchen Architekturkritiker zu der leicht ironischen Annahme verleitete, Meier selbst habe hier optimierend nachgebessert. Dem neuen Konzept dieses Cafés, aber auch der Neustrukturierung der Sammlungen zollte Meier selbst Beifall. Ebenso dem neu in der Museumslobby situierten Design-Shop, den, aufbauend auf Meiers doppelt an den Längsseiten der Lobby befindlichen Rezeptionen aus fest eingebauten Granit-Theken, ebenfalls Uwe Fischer gestaltet hat. Neben der Adaption einer der beiden fest installierten Verkaufstheken für die Bedürfnisse des Shops entwickelte Fischer demontable Präsentationsflächen, da bei Ausstellungseröffnungen und internen Veranstaltungen von Partner-Unternehmen die Lobby jeweils mit einer Reihenbestuhlung versehen wird. Sowohl die angebotenen Produkte im Shop als auch die gastronomischen Angebote im Café-Restaurant entsprechen und sind kompatibel mit den Sammlungen. So bietet der Museumsshop bewußt Produkte an, deren Qualität ihnen die Aufnahme in die ständige Designsammlung des Museums sicherte. Im Museumsshop ist Sehen nicht mehr »interesseloses Wohlgefallen«. Ohne die Möglichkeit zu kaufen, bleibt ein Museumsbesucher Flaneur. »Wenn es die Aufgabe des Museums ist«, schreibt James M. Bradburne im Katalog zur Ausstellung »I think, therefore I shop«, »die Entwicklung des kritischen Sehens zu fördern, so beginnt und endet der Museumsbesuch zweifellos bei der Frage nach dem Stellenwert des Einkaufens.« Jener Konnex zwischen historischer Erkenntnis, Erwerb und Genuß ist dem Museum für Angewandte Kunst ein besonderes Anliegen, denn was wäre wichtiger, als im Kosmos der Angebote Unterscheidungshilfen zu geben? Und wer wäre prädestinierter dazu als ein Museum für die Gegenstände des Gebrauchs, die zudem nach strengen ästhetischen und produktkulturellen Kriterien ausgewählt und präsentiert werden? Von der Anschauung zur Anwendung, vom Probieren zum Goutieren, von der historischen Sensibilität zur gegenwärtigen Sensualität. Das ist weder ahistorisch noch antiwissenschaftlich, denn die Unterfütterung durch die Wahrnehmung historischer Bedingtheiten potenziert die Entscheidungs- und Genußfähigkeit für das Hier und Heute.

Der Museumspark

Nach den Plänen des Architekten wurden an den Wegkreuzungen und Wegen des Parks hüfthohe weiße Leuchtstelen installiert. Nach über zehn Jahren Nutzungszeit dieser sehr ästhetischen Leuchten waren jedoch die Kosten der notwendigen Reparaturen aufgrund von Zerstörungen so immens, daß eine Alternative geboten schien. Darüber hinaus mieden die Anwohner den Park nach Einbruch der Dunkelheit, was den Vandalismus zusätzlich begünstigte. Aufgrund seiner freundschaftlichen Beziehung zu Ernesto Gismondi, dem Inhaber und CEO der italienischen Leuchtenfirma Artemide, erhielt das Museum von diesem 20 gut 4 m hohe Außenleuchten, die ein Tochterunternehmen von Artemide, die deutsche Firma DZ Licht, nach Entwürfen von Michele de Lucchi entwickelt hatte. Das Museum versteht diese »Palme«-Leuchten als Teil der ständigen Designsammlung des Hauses. Entsprechend ihrem Namen bestehen sie aus lackierten Metallrohren, an deren oberem Ende sich eine wie ein Löffel oder eine offene Hand gewölbte ovaloide Form anschließt, in deren Wölbung das Leuchtmittel sitzt. Die dunkelgraue Farbe dieser Leuchtstelen macht sie bei Nacht nahezu unsichtbar. Bei der Auswahl dieser Leuchten war Richard Meier involviert. Auch wenn die folgende Assoziation weit hergeholt erscheint:

3. Andersen Computer-Lab, 2000.
4. Kleinkinderspielplatz im Park des Museums, 2000; Entwurf und Ausführung: Efthymios Warlamis, Schrems, Österreich.

3. Andersen Computer Lab, 2000.
4. Playground for small children in the museum park, 2000; design and realisation: Efthymios Warlamis, Schrems, Austria.

as those of the present. Wednesday evening, entitled »spektakel« features guided tours by scholars or interactive theatre presentations by actors. The Thursday evening, entitled »conversazione« is devoted to giving the public an opportunity to handle selected museum objects as a means of promoting intensive discussion, while Friday evenings offer an exchange of ideas under the rubric »salon«. Finally, every first Saturday in the month the museum hosts »happy.hour« in which visitors can explore at first hand the »arts of the table«, using objects from the museum's collections and enjoy related activities such as wine tastings and special museum-related dinners.

The museum has also innovated in reaching younger audiences. In addition to its »Digital Craft« project, which attracts teenagers and young adults with exhibitions such as »I love you: Computers, Viruses, Hackers, and Culture« (2002), the museum also has a wide range of programmes and activities for families and children, including special children's labelling, a children's guide to the museum, interactive exhibits, and special »suitcases« to help families discover the treasures of the museum. Moreover, a special team of young art history students – the so-called mak.crew – is available to give information, advice, and even impromptu tours when asked by museum visitors.

Café-restaurant and museum shop

It is one of the necessities of a contemporary international museum to provide the opportunity to shop and to dine. From the outset, Meier's original concept included a restaurant with a capacity of about 200 seats both inside and on the terrace outside the building. Richard Meier furnished it in the style of a Viennese café. There was a counter for cakes and for salads, but notably neither a bar nor a lounge for casual reading and drinks during »happy hour«. This need was addressed during the re-positioning that was part of the »relaunch« of the museum in May 2000.

Today, the restaurant is not only a restaurant but also an extension of the museum's core mission – a place where the applied arts can be experienced in a more immediate way than when displayed in glass cases. The taste of an exquisite wine is best appreciated in a fine crystal goblet, and a lacquered Japanese bowl reveals new properties when it contains steaming pearl-like rice. Moreover, the restaurant hosts tastings of exquisite wines served in historical glasses as well as special dinners served on designer porcelain. In this sense, the restaurant is integrally related to the collections of the museum itself – the restaurant is in effect the »stage« on which the applied arts are »performed«.

The café-restaurant was completely remodeled by the Frankfurt architect and designer Uwe Fischer. A private dining room was added, a bar was installed, and the restaurant, bar, and bistro were clearly articulated. The restaurant's hours, previously limited to 7 p.m. were extended to midnight and beyond, thus prolonging the activity of the museum, itself now open daily until 8 p.m. The entire space, which was formerly carpeted and furnished with chairs in the style of a Viennese café was emptied and received a new appeal with a dark oak parquet floor, with chairs designed by the Belgian Gert van Severen, and with elegant warm grey leather seating. The newly installed architectural elements of the interior have given the room a new and characteristic image prompting several architectural critics to ironically suggest that Richard Meier had personally made some further improvements.

Meier was involved at every stage of the planning of the re-installation and applauded the new café concept as well as the re-structuring of the permanent collections. He was also involved in the design of the shop situated in the lobby of the museum, also designed by Uwe Fischer. Fischer's design incorporates Meier's granite double reception desks placed along either side of the lobby. In addition to the adaptation of one of the two reception desks to meet the demands of the shop, Fischer developed removable counters and display spaces, as the lobby must accommodate rows of seating during exhibition openings and events. Both the selection of articles in the shop and the display of objects from the museum's collections in the café-restaurant are inextricably related to the museum's mission.

This means that the museum shop explicitly sells objects that have been included in the museum's permanent collections, have been exhibited in the museum's temporary exhibitions or are of a quality that the museum would consider collecting. Exceptionally, in this museum shop the act of viewing is no longer just disinterested browsing, on the contrary, the act of buying an object is seen as part of the museum's educational strategy. Without the opportunity to buy, the visitor to the museum remains little more than a flâneur. In the catalogue to the exhibition »I think, therefore I shop«, James M. Bradburne wrote »If the museum's mission is to encourage the development of the skills of critical looking, surely the museum visit both begins and ends with shopping.« To the Museum for Applied Art, this relationship between historical knowledge, purchase, and enjoyment is a matter of special consideration. After all, what would be more important than to prepare visitors with new skills to help them make better decisions within a consumerist cosmos? And who is better suited to give such advice than a museum for the applied arts in which the articles have, after all, been selected and displayed according to the strict cultural criteria of aesthetics and of production? This thought leads from viewing to use, from dabbling to appreciation, from a historical sensibility to a present-day sensuality. This practice is neither a-historical nor anti-scientific, since strengthening our human perceptions in the area of historical truths easily leads to a potential for improved decision-making and the capacity for enjoyment in the here and now.

The museum park

According to the plans of the architect, waist-high lighting standards were erected at each intersection of the walkways. Unfortunately, by the year 2000, the cost of repairing these aesthetically beautiful lamps had become a burden due

Erinnert diese offene Form nicht an die geöffnete Hand Le Corbusiers, die dieser für seine Regierungsbauten in Candigarh/ Indien zum offiziellen Logo kreierte – und ist nicht andererseits Meier dem (Früh-)Werk Le Corbusiers besonders verpflichtet? Über Ecken mag man also eine innere Verwandtschaft zwischen Meier, Le Corbusier und De Lucchi konstatieren. Die Lichtleistung ist so stark, daß das Museum gegenüber der ursprünglichen Dichte der Leuchtpunkte nur noch jeden zweiten Punkt zu bestücken brauchte. Der Park mit diesen neuen Leuchten und seinen großen Grünflächen ist im Sommer ein beliebter Treffpunkt und wird von vielen zum Sonnen, zum langen »Brunch«-Aufenthalt auf der Terrasse des Café-Restaurants, für Spiel, Spaß und Erholung genutzt.

Eine weitere Neuerung im Park des Museums ist ein Kleinkinder-Spielplatz mit sehr farbigen, postmodern abstrahierten Tierskulpturen und Phantasieformen. Der austro-griechische Architekt, Designer und Künstler Efthymios Warlamis zeichnet dafür mit seinem Team verantwortlich, welches bereits ähnliche, weit größere Anlagen auch in Paris oder Athen realisiert hat. Die bunten, kindlich gestalteten, knubbeligen Krokodile und Giraffen, Nilpferde und Enten, eine kleine Rutsche und ein geheimnisvolles Pilzhaus entsprechen dem Erlebnismodus von 3- bis 7jährigen. Das Museum begreift diesen Kleinkinderspielplatz, der dank einem finanziellen Engagement der Wohnungsbaugesellschaft Nassauische Heimstätte möglich wurde, als weiteren Baustein in einem interaktiven Mix an Angeboten für seine Besucher.

Ausstellungsprogramm

Wie jedes Museum mit eigenen umfangreichen Sammlungen konzipiert auch das Museum für Angewandte Kunst in Frankfurt einige seiner jährlichen großen Wechselausstellungen aus eigenen Beständen. Hinzu kommen Sonderausstellungen mit Leihgaben aus aller Welt, die Epochen und Stile, Überblicke über das Werk einzelner Gestalter oder thematische Zusammenhänge zum Inhalt haben. Alle drei Jahre zeigt das Museum darüber hinaus eine »Triennale des zeitgenössischen Kunsthandwerks«, oft in Verbindung mit Partnerländern, z. B. Korea (1997), Australien (2000) oder den USA (2003). Daneben stehen Ausstellungsübernahmen, etwa vom New Yorker Museum of Modern Art, dem Van Gogh Museum in Amsterdam, dem Prager Museum für Angewandte Kunst oder dem Vitra Design Museum in Weil am Rhein. Dabei reicht die Bandbreite der Sonderausstellungen von japanischen Textilien (2001) oder chinesischer Keramik (2002) über Einzelausstellungen bedeutender zeitgenössischer Gestalter wie Ingo Maurer (2001), Richard Meier (2003), Dieter Rams (2001) oder Stefan Wewerka (1998) und Überblicken zu gegenwärtigen Entwurfshaltungen, etwa mit der Schau »13 nach Memphis« (1997), bis zu umfangreichen gattungsübergreifenden Ausstellungen wie »Blut: Perspektiven der Kunst, Macht, Politik und Pathologie«, die angewandte Kunst, klassische Malerei, aktuelle Kunst mit naturwissenschaftlichen, medizinischen und medizinhistorischen Fragestellungen verband. Ausstellungen wie »Prag um 1900« (2000) oder zum österreichischen »K & K-Produktkabinett« (1996) thematisierten spezielle Kulturräume und Metropolen, dazu gehören Schauen über zeitgenössische Schmuck- und Buchkünstler, über Buchkunst und Buchbinden in der Barockabteilung und über Kalligraphie in der Islam-Abteilung. In sogenannten »Interventionen« in den ständigen Sammlungen vernetzt das Museum Themen der Sonderausstellungen mit seinen Beständen; in kleinen »Fragebogen«-Ausstellungen werden die Besucher aufgefordert, unbeschriftet ausgestellte Objekte unter verschiedenen Gesichtspunkten zu bewerten, und finden auf der Website des Museums die Auflösung der Fragen wie etwa: Welches der ausgestellten Objekte ist eine Fälschung, oder: welche Objekte wurden von Frauen gestaltet?

5. »13 nach Memphis. Design zwischen Askese und Sinnlichkeit«, 1995.
6. »Lust und Verlust im britischen Design heute«, 1999.
7. »Über allen Gipfeln ... Naturerfahrung zwischen Goethe und Gegenwart«, 1999.
8. »Blut: Perspektiven der Kunst, Macht, Politik und Pathologie«, 2001.
9. »Struktur und Oberfläche. Japanische Textilien heute«, 2001.

5. »13 after Memphis. Design between Asceticism and Sensuality«, 1995.
6. »Lost and Found, Critical Voices in British Design«, 1999.
7. »Overall the Hill-Tops ... Experiencing Nature from Goethe's Time to the Present«, 1999.
8. »Blood: Perspectives of Art, Power, Politics, and Pathology«, 2001.
9. »Structure and Surface. Contemporary Japanese Textiles«, 2001.

to increased vandalism that an alternative type of lighting had to developed. Moreover, the low lighting levels in the park discouraged local residents from using the park after dark, further encouraging vandalism. The solution came from Ernesto Gismondi, the owner and CEO of the Italian lighting firm Artemide, who donated 20 exterior lights of almost four meters in height to the museum. Produced by a subsidiary of Artemide, the German firm DZ-Licht and designed by Michele De Lucchi, the museum considers these »palm-shaped« lamps as an integral part of its permanent design collection. As their name suggests, they consist of lacquered metal piping which spreads at the upper extremity into »palm«-shaped rounded, oval forms. These »leaves«, in turn, capture and reflect the light. The deep grey colour of the lamp's »stems«, which makes them almost invisible at night, was chosen in collaboration with Richard Meier. The following association may appear far-fetched but does this not remind one of Le Corbusier's »open hand«, which he used as the official logo of his governmental building structures in Chandigarh, India? And is Meier not especially indebted to Le Corbusier in his early work? One may, then, be allowed to note a distant relationship between Meier, Le Corbusier, and De Lucchi. The lamps are so effective that the museum only needed to use half as many as originally planned. With new lighting and amenities the park with its large green open spaces has become a favorite meeting place for many Frankfurt residents. It certainly is much in use for enjoying the sun, games, fun, and relaxation, as well as for leisurely »brunch« on the terrace of the café-restaurant.

Another innovation in the park of the museum is a small children's playground. The colorful and somewhat abstract animal-shaped or other phantastical structures are the product of the imagination of the Greco-Austrian architect, designer, and artist Efthymios Warlamis and his team. They have already designed much larger projects in Paris and Athens. The colorful crocodiles with their pudgy, childlike quality, the giraffes, hippos and ducks, as well as a small slide and a mysterious mushroom-shaped house correspond to the experience and educational needs of three-to-five-year olds. Sponsored by the local housing developer the Nassauische Heimstätte this playground is an additional building block in a mix of activities the museum offers to an increasingly broad spectrum of visitors.

Exhibition program

Like every museum with own extensive holdings the Frankfurt Museum for Applied Art builds many of its major annual exhibitions around objects in its own permanent collections. In addition, the museum organises special exhibitions containing loans from museums around the world. The museum also hosts exhibitions which offer overviews of the work of individual designers or exhibitions with interrelated themes. Moreover, the very three years the museum organizes a »triennial exhibition of contemporary arts and crafts«. This exhibition is organized in conjunction with international partners, which have included museums in countries such as Korea (1997), Australia (2000), and the USA (2003). The museum also hosts exhibitions organized by other museums, such as the New York Museum of Modern Art, the Van Gogh Museum in Amsterdam, the Museum of Decorative Arts in Prague or the Vitra Design Museum at Weil am Rhein. The thematic breadth of special programmes spans Japanese textiles (2001) or Chinese ceramics (2002) to the works of individual artists like Ingo Maurer (2001), Richard Meier (2003), Dieter Rams (2001), or Stefan Wewerka (1998). The museum organises general overview displays of contemporary tendencies in design, such as the exhibition »13 after Memphis« (1997), as well as much larger interdisciplinary exhibitions such as »Blood: Perspectives of Art, Power, Politics, and Pathology« (2001) connecting applied art, fine art and con-

Internationale Gastkuratoren wie Edwin Becker, James Clifton, Jonathan Miller, Murray Moss, Miri Rubin oder Harriet Watts bereichern die Fragestellungen des Museums mit eigenen, spannenden Installationen. Regelmäßige Vorträge von externen Experten oder den Wissenschaftlern des Hauses vertiefen die Themen der Sonderausstellungen.

Nachhaltige Finanzierung des Museums durch Partnerschaften

Es ist sowohl eine Frage der ökonomischen Vernunft als auch der Planungssicherheit, wenn bei zurückgehenden öffentlichen Mitteln Museen Drittmittelfinanzierungen forcieren, die über punktuelles Sponsoring hinausgehen. Neben solchem Sponsoring für Sonderausstellungen hat das Museum für Angewandte Kunst deshalb in den letzten Jahren gezielt Partner aus der Industrie für jeweils drei Jahre gesucht und gefunden. James Bradburne, der Direktor des Museums während dieser Phase, hat oft mit leichter Provokation gesagt: »Wir wollen keine Sponsoren – wir wollen Partner.« Das Museum war besonders dann erfolgreich im Werben um Partner, wenn deren eigene Unternehmensphilosophie mit den Zielen des Museums übereinstimmte. Ein Unternehmen wie z.B. Nokia, das sich als Ziel gesteckt hat, »Leute zu verbinden« (Connecting people), fühlt sich dem Museum verbunden, welches eine »piazza«, ein Ort der Begegnung sein will. Mit solchen Partnern kann das Museum über einen längeren Zeitraum gemeinsam Projekte entwickeln und finanzieren. Dies ist besonders für das Forschungsprojekt »Digital Craft« wichtig, welches nur durch die Hilfe von Firmen wie Arthur Andersen, Apple, Deutsche Telekom, Nokia und seine Microsystems möglich wurde. Die umfangreichen pädagogischen Programme des Museums, zu denen Führungen in türkisch, längere Öffnungszeiten, die »mak.crew« und jenes populäre Programm gehören, das auf den »Mindstorm«-Robotern von Lego basiert sowie die Kurse im Programm »Robo.mak«, wurden durch diverse Partnerschaften mit der Nassauischen Heimstätte, Clifford Chance Pünder, der Messe Frankfurt, der Deutschen Börse, der *Frankfurter Allgemeinen Zeitung*, J.P. Morgan Chase und Braun ermöglicht. Weitere wichtige Partner sind die Werbeagentur Publicis, die Public Relations Agentur Britta Fischer und das Kunsttransportunternehmen Schenker. Diese mannigfaltigen Kooperationen verdichten die museologische Erfahrung und Praxis, transzendieren sie aber auch. So produzierte das Museum etwa mit Hilfe der Unternehmen Lego und J.P. Morgan Chase und in Kooperation mit dem Ballett Frankfurt am Main und seinem Choreographen William Forsythe ein Projekt, welches später auf dem Festival »Third World Summit for Media & Children« in Thessaloniki aufgeführt und weltweit über CCN ausgestrahlt wurde. In diesem Projekt halfen Bill Forsythe, die Tänzerin Ana Roman und der Pädagoge Paul Kaiser den Kindern, den Charakter ihrer eigenen Bewegungen zu entdecken, den sie dann in Bewegungen von Lego-Robotern »übersetzten«. Die Kinder kreierten somit ihre eigene Aufführung, in der sie mit den Robotern tanzend kooperierten, die sie selbst zusammengebaut und programmiert hatten.

James M. Bradburne, der Direktor des Hauses in dieser Phase der neuen Orientierung und Fokussierung, hat dies mit zwei Sentenzen auf den Punkt gebracht: »Das Museum sollte eine Piazza, nicht ein Stadion sein«, ein Ort der Begegnung, der Interaktion, des informellen Lernens und Austauschens und nicht einfach nur eine »Veranstaltungsmaschine« mit angehängten Ausstellungen – und mit dem, nur auf den ersten Blick, irritierenden Ausspruch: »Wir wollen nicht nur Besucher, wir wollen Benutzer!«, weil ein Museum seinen Erfolg daran messen sollte, ob seine Besucher immer wiederkommen. Jenseits aller rhetorischen Zuspitzung umreißen diese beiden Aussagen die Chancen und die Probleme heutigen Museumsmanagements.

Resümee

Aus der Beschreibung der unterschiedlichen Aktivitäten wird deutlich, daß das Museum für Angewandte Kunst in Frankfurt am Main sich die Überprüfung der traditionellen Museums-Paradigmen zum Ziel gesetzt hat. Es ist ein Ort der Belehrung und Erbauung, ein Ort der Begegnung und Kommunikation mit dem vielfältigen Reichtum vergangener und gegenwärtiger Produkte. Es geht um den Erwerb von Unterscheidungsfähigkeit und das Erkennen von Qualität von Produkten und Konzepten, um die Steigerung der Fähigkeiten, kritisches Engagement mit der Kultur der Gegenwart zu verknüpfen. Es geht darum, die historisch wechselnden Bedingungen für Kreativität, Ästhetik und Schönheit zu verstehen und aus heutiger Sicht zu interpretieren. Dabei betrachtet das Museum seine Besucher als aktive Teilnehmer seiner Fragestellungen und forciert selbstverständlich auch die Vermittlung streng fachwissenschaftlicher Ergebnisse und Forschungen. Das Panorama von Gebrauchsgegenständen höchsten künstlerischen und kulturellen Niveaus reicht dabei von jahrtausendealter chinesischer Keramik bis zum mittelalterlichen Elfenbein-Reisealtar, von antiken türkischen Teppichen bis zur Überfang-Glasvase von Emile Gallé, von Thonets Caféhausstuhl bis zur Swatch-Armbanduhr, von barocken Wandteppichen bis zum WAP-Mobiltelefon: all dies und mehr, damit, wie Friedrich Schiller sagte, »der Mensch sich nicht selbst versäume«.

temporary art with the questions and problems of the natural sciences, the history of medicine and political philosophy. Other exhibitions such as »Prague 1900« (2000) or »K&K Product Cabinet« (1996) are concerned with specific cultural fields or capital cities.

In its so-called »Interventions«, which are special displays within the museum's permanent collections, the museum connects themes of its special exhibitions with those of its regular holdings. Interventions include shows about contemporary jewelry design in the permanent collection of 20th century craft, book art, and bookbinding in the Baroque collection, and calligraphy in the Islamic collection themes. In the area known as »Questionnaire«, visitors are asked to give their opinion on un-labelled objects assembled from various points of view. For instance, which of the objects displayed is a fake? Or which objects were designed by women? They can then find a discussion of the issues raised on the museum's website. To bring an international dimension to the museum's exhibitions, guest curators, such as Edwin Becker, James Clifton, Jonathan Miller, Murray Moss, Miri Rubin, and Harriet Watts, come to enrich the museum with their own exciting contributions. Regular lectures by outside experts or by the museum's curators add depth to these special exhibitions.

Sustainable funding of the museum through partnerships

At a time of shrinking public support it becomes as much a question of economic reasoning as one of security of planning when museums are forced to find financial means from third parties, often going much beyond isolated sponsorship of single exhibitions. Besides the usual sponsors, during the past few years the Museum for Applied Art has aimed specifically to find three-year partners in industry. James Bradburne, the museum's director during this phase, often says provocatively »we don't want sponsors – we want partners«. The museum has been especially successful attracting partners who can identify their own business philosophy with the goals of the museum. A firm like Nokia, for instance, whose stated mission is »connecting people«, has no problem supporting a museum whose public goal is to be a »piazza«. With a simple sponsorship, the support is limited to a pre-defined event such as an exhibition. With a three-year partner, the museum can develop and finance important projects over some length of time. This has been especially important for the research project »Digital Craft« which was only possible through the help of firms such as Arthur Andersen, Apple, Deutsche Telekom, Nokia, and Sun Microsystems. The extensive educational programmes developed by the museum, including programmes in Turkish, longer opening hours, the »mak.crew« and the popular programme based on LEGO's »Mindstorms« robots, ROBO.mak, were made possible by the partnerships of the Nassauische Heimstätte, Clifford Chance Pünder, the Messe Frankfurt, the Deutsche Börse, the Frankfurter Allgemeine Zeitung, J. P. Morgan Chase, and Braun. Other significant partners included the advertising agency Publicis, Britta Fischer Public Relations and Schenker Deutschland.

These many-faceted collaborations condense in some sense museological experience and practice, indeed, they also transcend it. For example, the museum worked with LEGO and J. P. Morgan as well as the Frankfurt Ballet and its choreographer William Forsythe to create a project that was later featured at the »Third World Summit for Media & Children« in Thessaloniki and broadcast across the world by CNN. In this project, Bill Forsythe, dancer Ana Roman and educator Paul Kaiser helped children explore the nature of their own movements, which they then »translated« into LEGO robots. The children then created their own performance, in which they »danced« with the robots they themselves had designed and programmed.

James M. Bradburne, the director of the museum during the relaunch process, summed up the museum's vision pertinently in two statements. The first declares that »the museum should be a piazza, not a stadium« that is the place of encounter, of interaction, and of informal learning and exchange, rather than an event-driven exhibition hall. The second is at first glance a provocation to the public, namely that »the museum doesn't want visitors, it wants users« – a place whose success can only be measured by the numbers who decide to return again and again. Beyond their pointed directness, both of these slogans also poignantly outline the opportunities as well as the challenges faced by the museum management of today.

Summary

From the description of the various activities it becomes apparent that the Museum for Applied Art in Frankfurt am Main aims at a complete re-examination of the traditional museum paradigm. It aims be a place for education and edification, as well as for an encounter and engagement with the many riches from past ages and from our own time. The central concern is to support the visitor's ability to distinguish and to recognise the quality of both objects and ideas, her capacity for critical engagement with contemporary culture. This means learning to comprehend from today's point of view and to interpret the changing historical conditions for creativity, aestheticism, and beauty. In this educational experience, the Museum sees its visitors as active participants in creating new knowledge, while it encourages them to engage with serious scholarly analysis and research. The museum's collection of objects of the highest artistic and cultural level extends from thousand-year old Chinese ceramics to the ivory travel altars of the Middle Ages, from antique Turkish carpets to the glass vases of Emile Gallé, from the coffee house chair of Thonet to the Swatch wrist-watch, from Baroque tapestries to WAP-mobile phones: all of this and more in order that, in the words of Friedrich Schiller, »Man may not miss himself«.

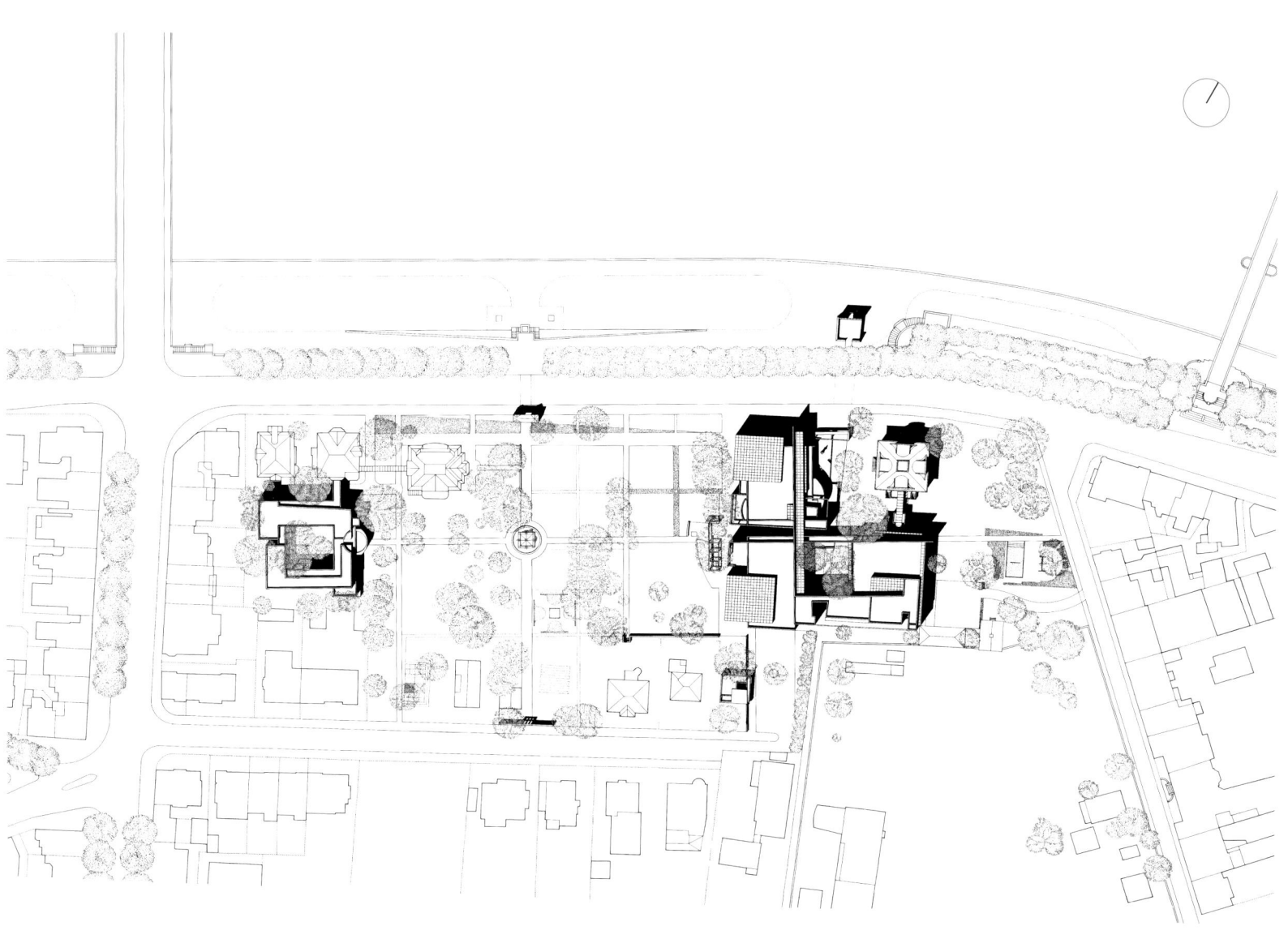

1. Lageplan.
2. Axonometrie des Gebäudes.
3. Axonometrie des Gebäudes mit Einblick in das 1. Obergeschoß.

1. Site plan.
2. Axonometric view of the building.
3. Axonometric view of the building with insight into the 1st floor.

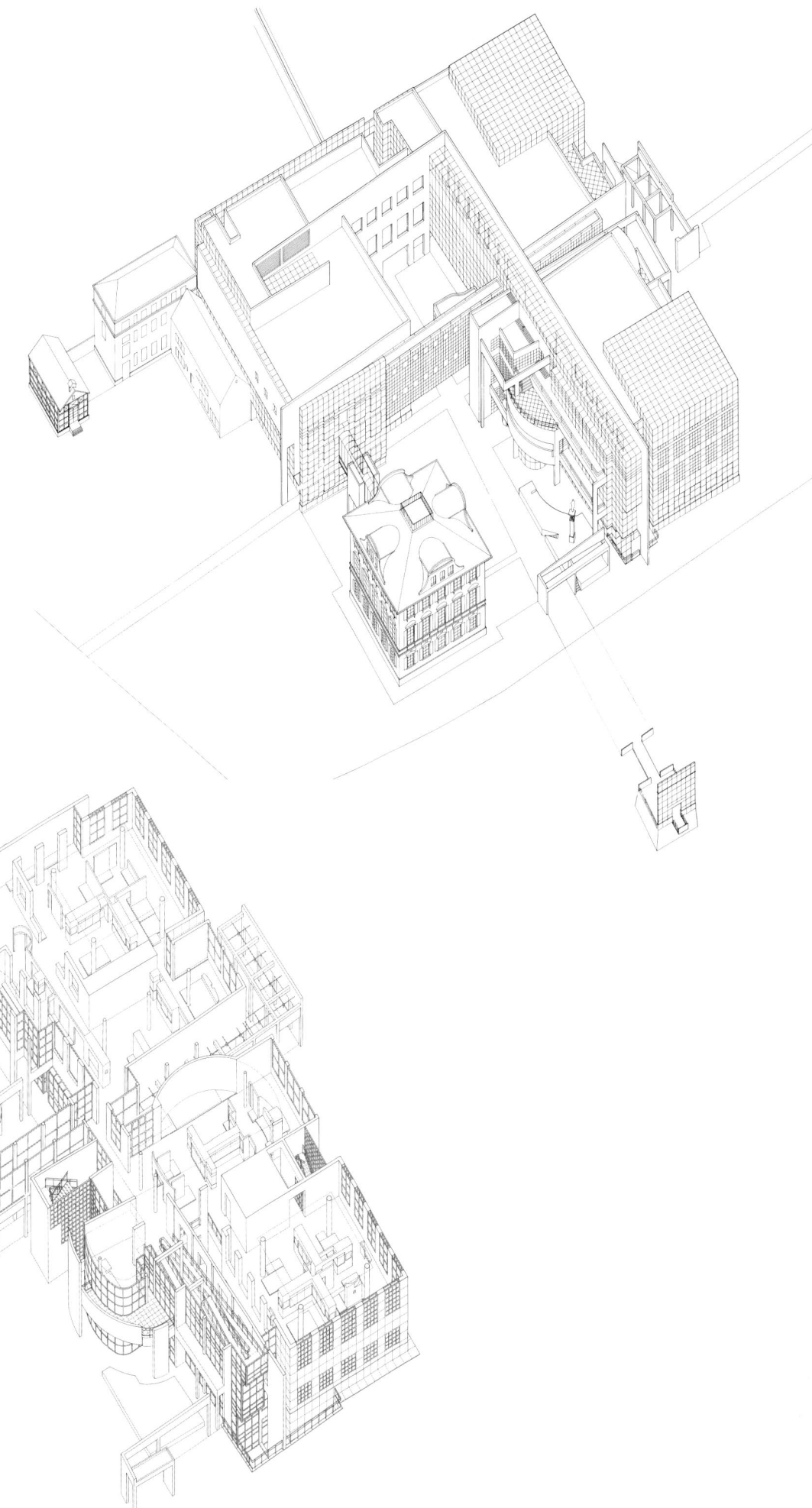

4, 5. Grundrisse (Untergeschoß, Erdgeschoß).

4, 5. Floor plans (basement, ground floor).

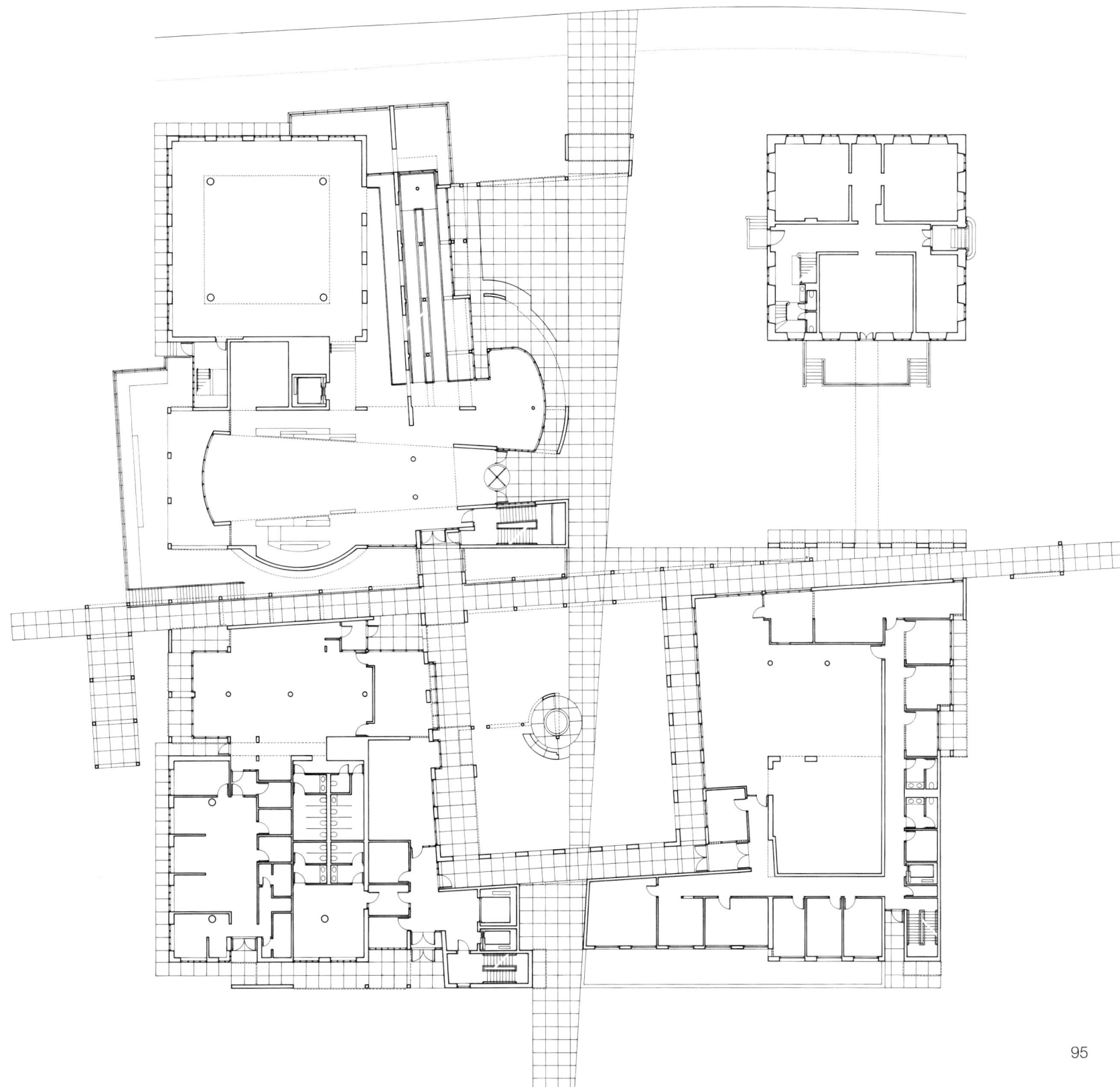

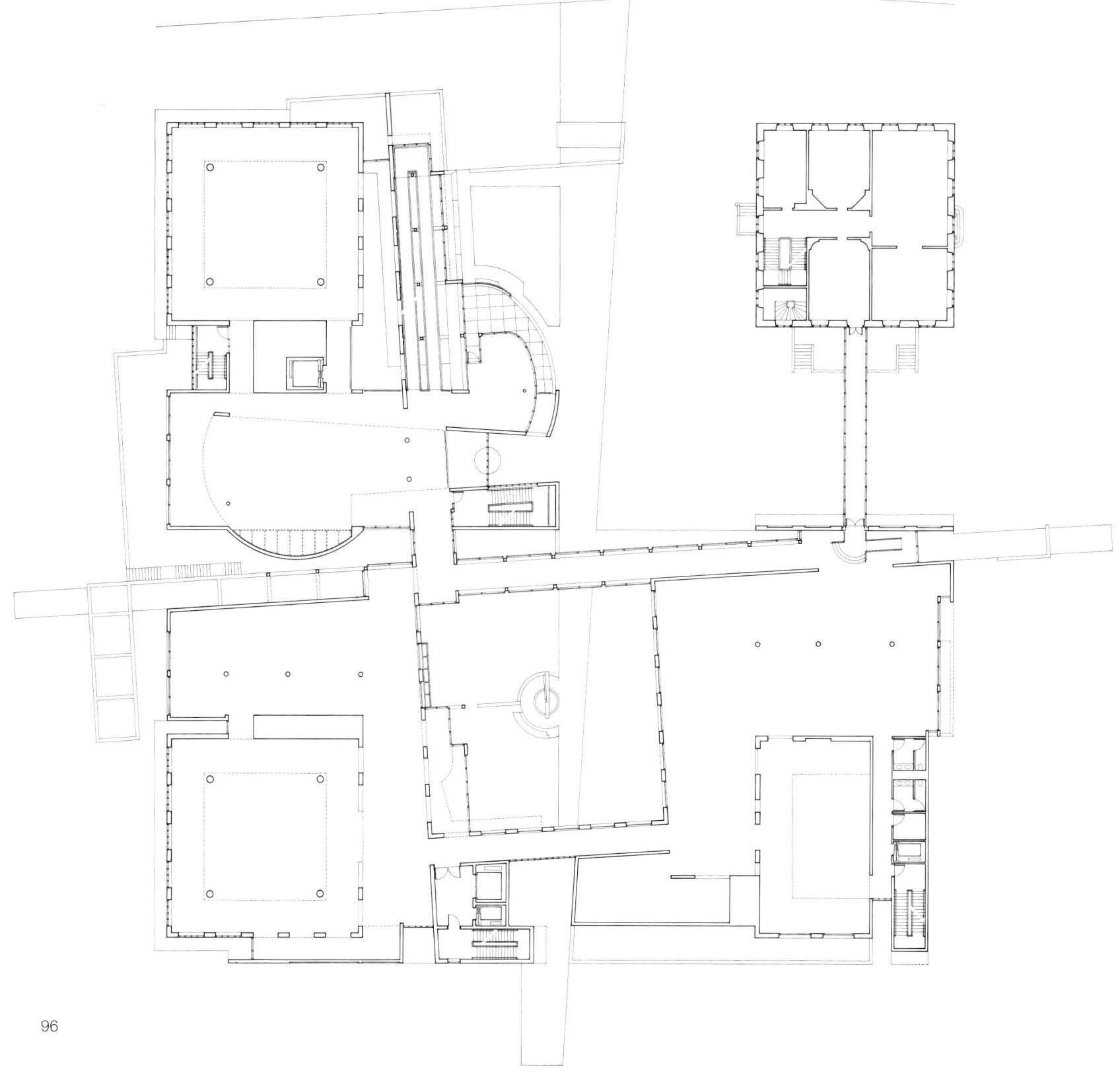

6, 7. Grundrisse (1. Obergeschoß, 2. Obergeschoß).

6, 7. Floor plans (1st floor, 2nd floor).

S. 98, 99
8, 9. Schnitte.

p. 98, 99
8, 9. Sections.

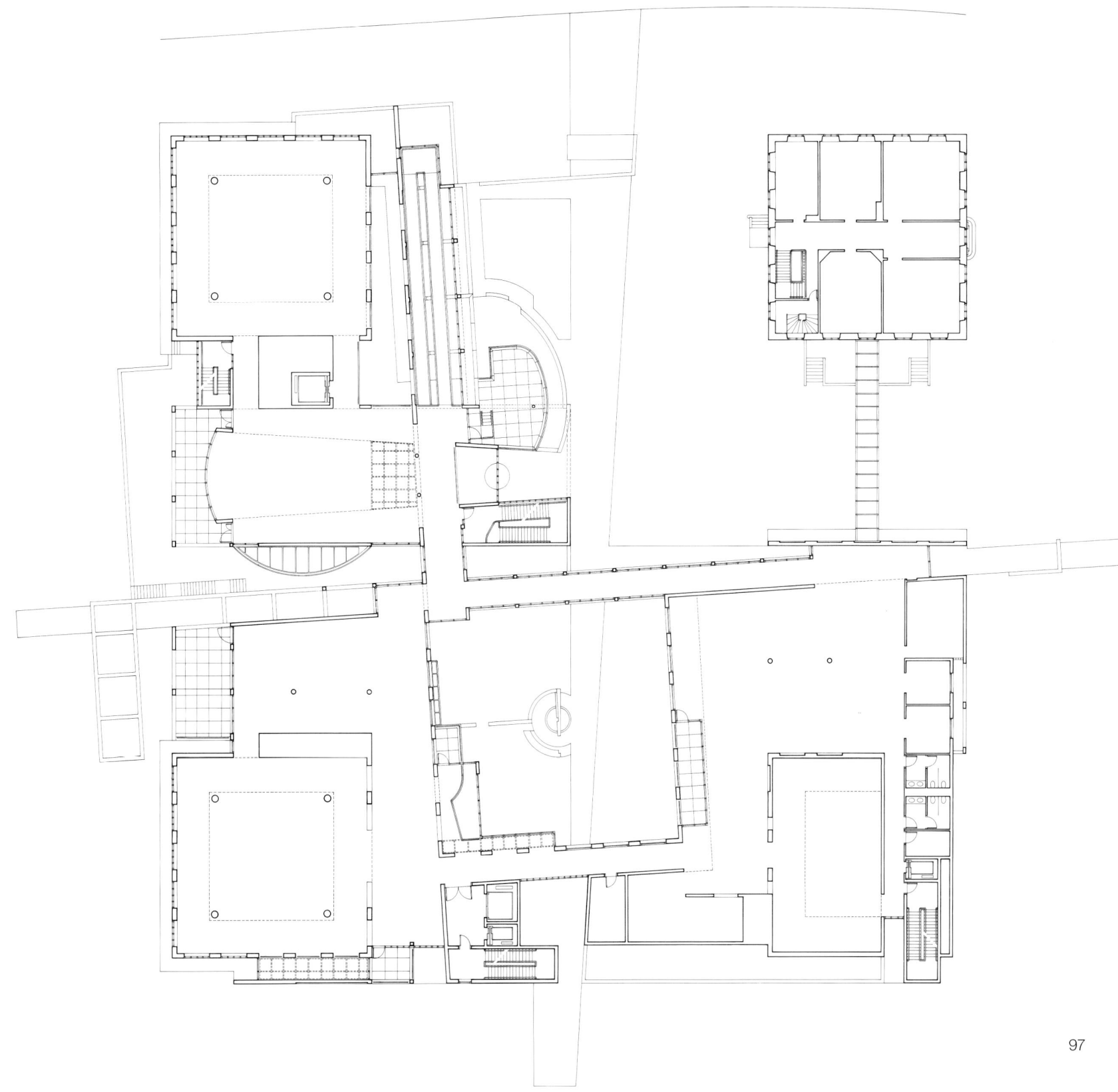

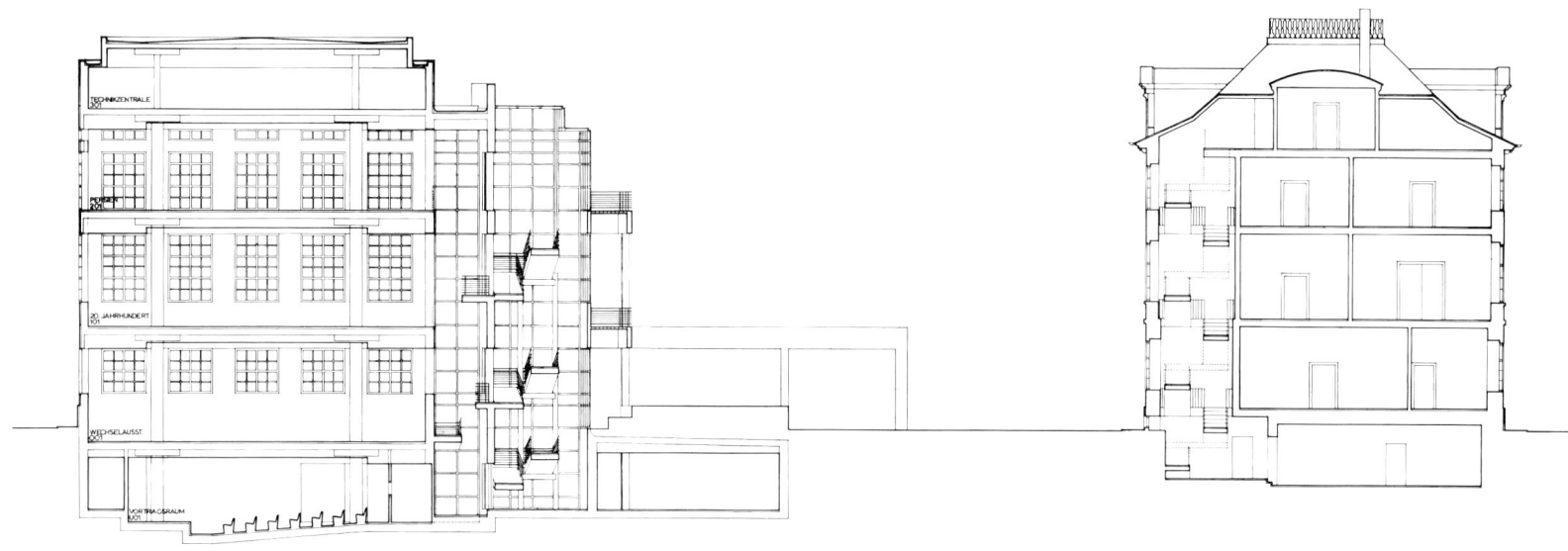
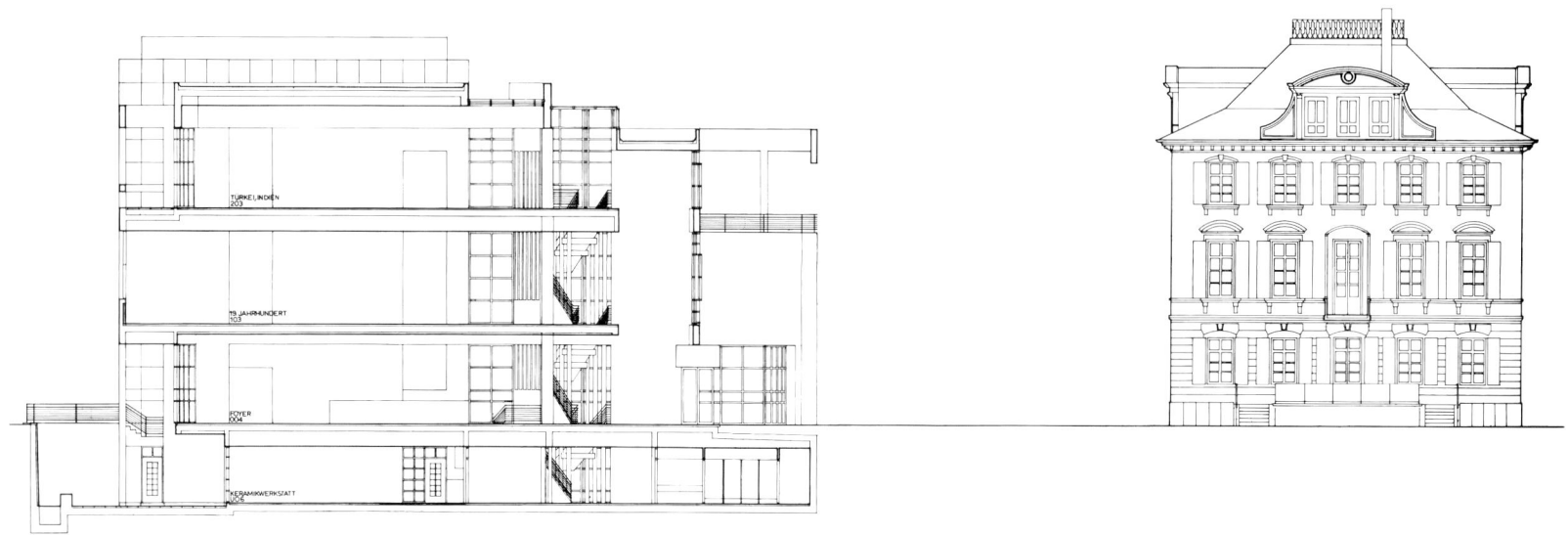
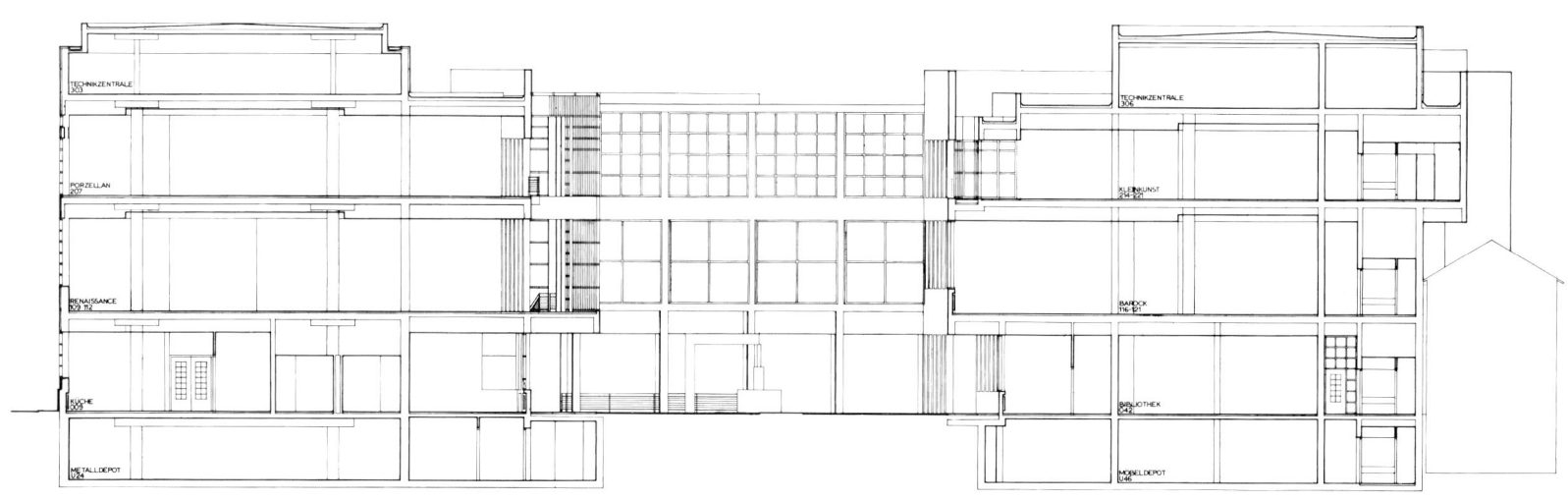

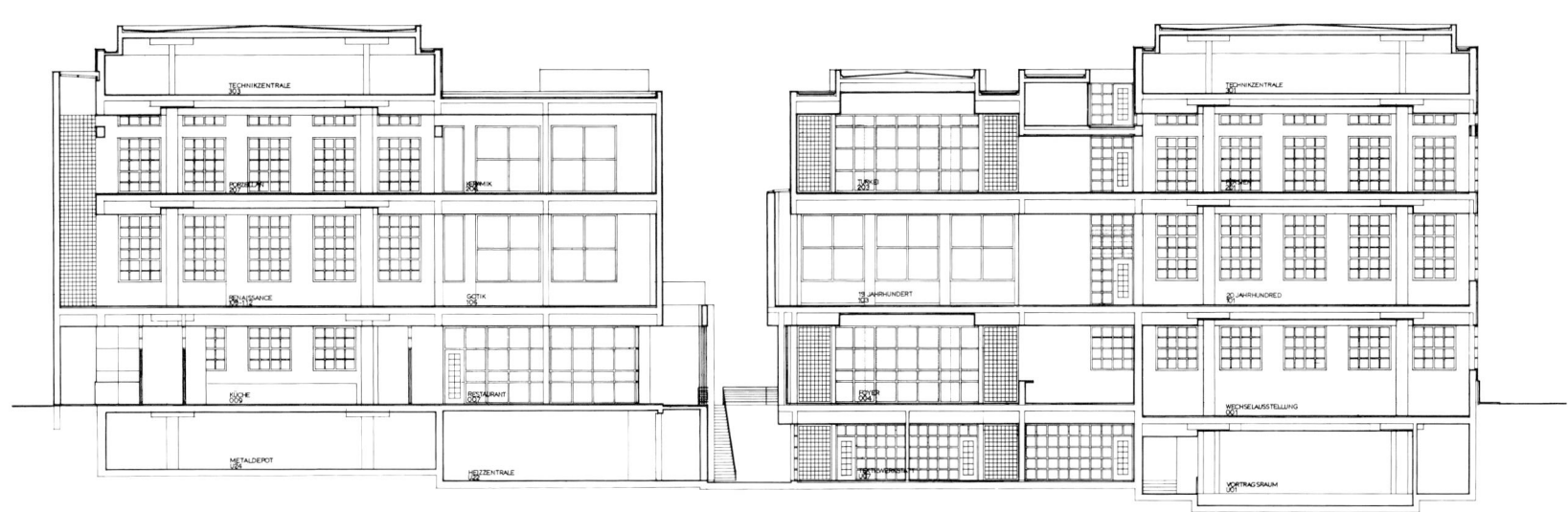
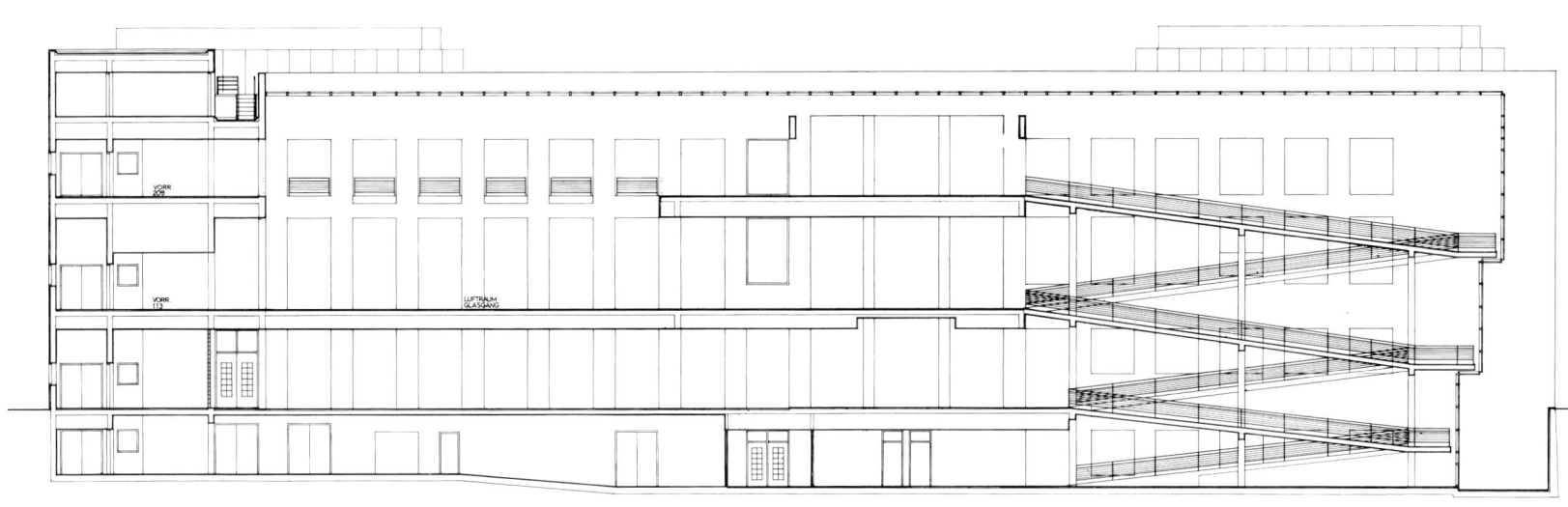
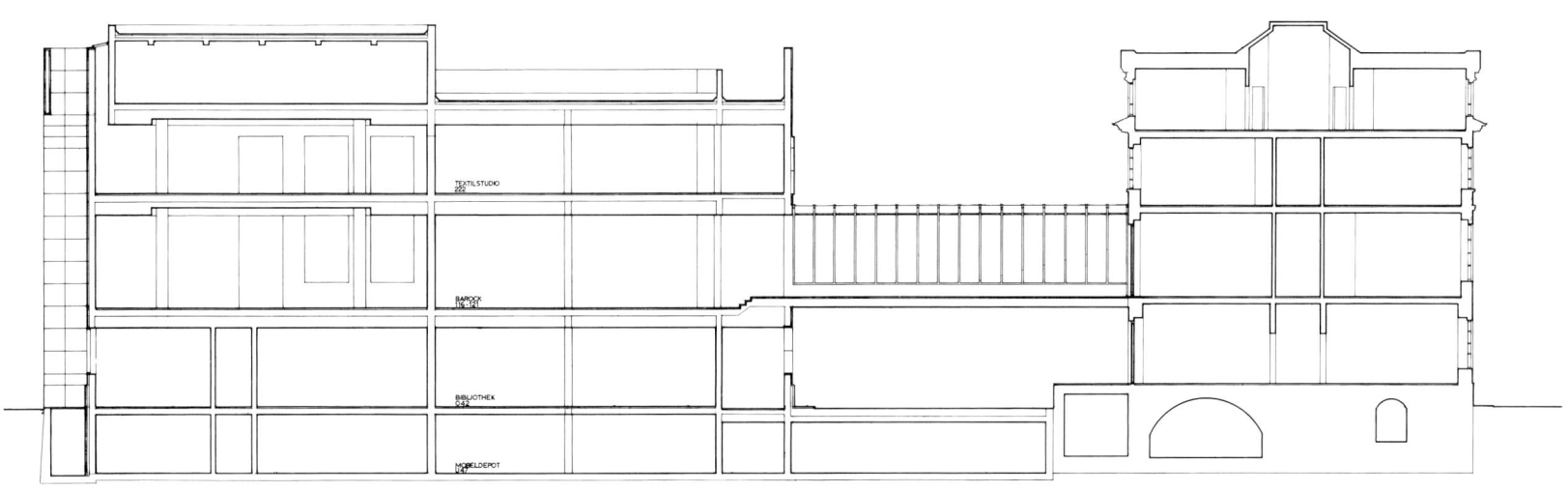

1. Luftansicht des Gebäudes.
2. Blick von der Straße auf die Eingangsseite.
3. Blick von der Villa Metzler auf die Eingangseite.

1. Aerial view of the building.
2. View of the entrance side from the street.
3. View of the entrance side from the Villa Metzler.

4. Der Museumsshop.
5. Die Rampe.

4. The museum shop.
5. The ramp.

6, 7. Die Abteilung Japan.

6, 7. The Japan section.

8–10. Die Abteilung China.

8–10. The China section.

11–13. Die Abteilung Islam.

11–13. The Islam section.

14–16. Die Abteilung Mittelalter.

14–16. The Middle Ages section.

17, 18. Die Abteilung Renaissance.

17, 18. The Renaissance section.

19–21. Die Abteilung Barock.

19–21. The Baroque section.

22–24. Die Abteilung Jugendstil.

22–24. The Art Nouveau section.

25–27. Die Abteilung 20. Jahrhundert.

25–27. The 20th-century section.

28–30. Die Abteilung Design.

28–30. The design section.

31–33. Das Café-Restaurant.

31–33. The café-restaurant.

34, 35. Der Museumspark.

34, 35. The museum park.

Anmerkungen

[1] In Wagners Zeichnung posieren die Figuren vor einer Automobilausstellung, stehen also für moderne Menschen. Vgl.: Otto Wagner, *Die Baukunst unserer Zeit*, 4. Aufl., Wien 1914, S. 34 ff.
[2] Zit. nach: Annette Tapert, *Swid Powell. Objects by Architects*, New York 1990, S. 73.
[3] Richard Meier, »Wo steht die Kunst der Architektur?«, in: *Der Architekt*, 1985, Nr. 3, S.109.
[4] Vgl.: Oswald Spengler, *Der Untergang des Abendlandes* (1918–22), München 1963, sowie Gustav René Hocke, *Die Welt als Labyrinth. Manier und Manie in der europäischen Kunst*, Hamburg 1957.
[5] Zit. nach: Arthur Lubow, »Der Meier der Moderne«, in: *AD Architectural Digest* (München), Oktober/November 2002, S. 54.
[6] Vgl.: Thomas Mann, *Der Zauberberg*, Berlin 1924.
[7] Vgl.: Marcel Proust, *Jean Santeuil*, Paris 1952; deutsch: Frankfurt am Main 1965.
[8] Vgl. Friedrich Nietzsche, »Vom Nutzen und Nachteil der Historie für das Leben«, in: Friedrich Nietzsche, *Werke*, hg. von G. Colli und M. Montinari, Berlin 1967 ff.
[9] Vgl. Volker Fischer, *Die Liege LC4 von Le Corbusier, Pierre Jeanneret und Charlotte Perriand*, Frankfurt am Main 1997.
[10] Otl Aicher, »greifen und begreifen«, in: *analog und digital*, Berlin 1991, S. 19.
[11] Annette Tapert, *Swid Powell. Objects by Architects*, New York 1990, bes. S. 72–81. Hier werden auch detailliert die Gründungsbedingungen des Unternehmens beschrieben: mental, stilistisch und ökonomisch.
[12] Ebd., S. 25.
[13] Ebd., S. 25.
[14] Ebd., S. 74.
[15] In leichter Überarbeitung zit. nach: Arnold Gehlen, »Heimweh, genannt Nostalgie«, *Die Presse* (Wien), 19.7 1975, S. 15.
[16] Ebd.
[17] »Foreword«, in: Lois Nesbitt, *Richard Meier Collage*, New York und London 1990, S. 6 f.
[18] »Introduction«, in: Lois Nesbitt, *Richard Meier. Sculpture: 1992–94*, New York 1994, S. 5 ff.
[19] Kenneth Frampton, »Richard Meiers Museum für Kunsthandwerk«, in: *Museum für Kunsthandwerk Frankfurt am Main*, Frankfurt 1985 (*Schriftenreihe des Hochbauamtes zu Bauaufgaben der Stadt Frankfurt am Main*), S. 46.
[20] Norbert Huse, »›Öffentlicher Kontext‹ und ›urbane Struktur‹ – Richard Meier in Frankfurt am Main«, in: *Richard Meier. Museum für Kunsthandwerk Frankfurt am Main*, Berlin 1985, S. 16.
[21] Ebd., S. 16.
[22] Richard Meier, »Architect's Statement«, in: *Museum für Kunsthandwerk Frankfurt am Main, 1985*, a.a.O., S. 63.
[23] Richard Meier, »Wo steht die Kunst der Architektur?«, *Der Architekt* (Stuttgart), 1985, Nr. 3, S. 109.
[24] Richard Meier, in: *Richard Meier. Architect*, New York 1984, S. 270.
[25] Vgl.: *mak.frankfurt*, München, London und New York 2001 (*Prestel Museumsführer Compact*).

Notes

[1] In Wagner's drawing the figures are posing in front of an automobile exhibition, so they stand for modern men. Cf.: Otto Wagner, *Die Baukunst unserer Zeit*, 4th ed., Vienna, 1914, pp. 34 ff.
[2] Quoted from: Annette Tapert, *Swid Powell. Objects by Architects*, New York, 1990, p. 73.
[3] Richard Meier, »Wo steht die Kunst der Architektur?«, in: *Der Architekt*, 1985, no. 3, p.109.
[4] Cf.: Oswald Spengler, *Der Untergang des Abendlandes* (1918–22), Munich, 1963, as well as Gustav René Hocke, *Die Welt als Labyrinth. Manier und Manie in der europäischen Kunst*, Hamburg, 1957.
[5] Quoted from: Arthur Lubow, »Der Meier der Moderne«, in: *AD Architectural Digest* (Munich), October/November 2002, p. 54.
[6] Cf.: Thomas Mann, *Der Zauberberg*, Berlin, 1924.
[7] Cf.: Marcel Proust, *Jean Santeuil*, Paris 1952; English: New York, 1979.
[8] Cf.: Friedrich Nietzsche, »Vom Nutzen und Nachteil der Historie für das Leben«, in: Friedrich Nietzsche, *Werke*, ed. by G. Colli und M. Montinari, Berlin, 1967 ff.
[9] Cf.: Volker Fischer, *The LC4 Chaise Longue by Le Corbusier, Pierre Jeanneret and Charlotte Perriand*, Frankfurt am Main, 1997.
[10] Otl Aicher, »graping with the hand and mind«, in: *analogous and digital*, Berlin, 1994, p. 20.
[11] Annette Tapert, *Swid Powell. Objects by Architects*, New York, 1990, esp. pp. 72–81. Here also the condition of the foundation are described: mentally, stilistically und economically.
[12] Ibid., p. 25.
[13] Ibid., p. 25.
[14] Ibid., p. 74.
[15] Quoted slightly revised from: Arnold Gehlen, »Heimweh, genannt Nostalgie«, *Die Presse*, Vienna, 19 July 1975, p. 15.
[16] Ibid.
[17] »Foreword«, in: Lois Nesbitt, *Richard Meier Collage*, New York and London, 1990, pp. 6 f.
[18] »Introduction«, in: Lois Nesbitt, *Richard Meier. Sculpture: 1992–94*, New York, 1994, pp. 5 ff.
[19] Kenneth Frampton, »Richard Meier's Museum für Kunsthandwerk«, in: *Museum für Kunsthandwerk Frankfurt am Main*, Frankfurt, 1985 (*Schriftenreihe des Hochbauamtes zu Bauaufgaben der Stadt Frankfurt am Main*), p. 51.
[20] Norbert Huse, »›Public context‹ and ›urban fabric‹ – Richard Meier in Frankfurt am Main«, in: *Richard Meier. Museum für Kunsthandwerk Frankfurt am Main*, Berlin, 1985, p. 17.
[21] Ibid., p. 17.
[22] Richard Meier, »Architect's Statement«, in: *Museum für Kunsthandwerk Frankfurt am Main*, 1985, op. cit., p. 63.
[23] Richard Meier, »Wo steht die Kunst der Architektur?«, *Der Architekt* (Stuttgart), 1985, no. 3, p. 109.
[24] Richard Meier, in: *Richard Meier. Architect*, New York, 1984, p. 270.
[25] Cf.: *mak.frankfurt*, Munich, London and New York, 2001 (*Prestel Museumsführer Compact*).

Danksagung

Ich möchte folgenden Personen und Firmen für ihre Unterstützung und ihr Engagement bei der Realisierung dieser Unternehmung danken:

Richard Meier und den Mitarbeitern seines Büros in New York, besonders Lisetta Koe, die die Organisation des Projektes mit größter Umsicht betrieb, sowie auch Esther Kim und Elizabeth Lee;

allen Herstellerfirmen, die Beiträge geleistet haben – Adrian Olabuenaga von Acme Studios, Dr. Alberto Alessi Anghini und Francesca Appiani von Alessi Spa, Arabia (hier Stefan Ytterborn und Mia Hesselgren von Ytterborn & Fuentes sowie Denise Costantino von Designor, Inc.), Dan Baldinger und Katherine Wildt von Louis Baldinger & Sons, Inc., Carlo Valli und Marinella Formenti von Fusital (Valli & Valli), Rud. Ibach Sohn, Andrew Cogan und Peter Cogan von Knoll International, Jack Markuse von Markuse, Cleto Munari, Alessandro Munari und Valentina Nardi von Cleto Munari, Alan Buff von Reed & Barton, Patricia Marti von Steuben, John Longfellow und Mark Walters von Stow Davis sowie Nan Swid von Swid Powell;

dem Frankfurter Bankhaus Hauck & Aufhäuser für sein finanzielles Engagement;

der Spedition Schenker Deutschland AG, Kelsterbach;

Axel Menges und Dorothea Duwe und ihrem Team für diese hervorragende Publikation – die erste über das Museum seit mehreren Jahren;

und schließlich meinen Kollegen im Museum, sowohl den ständigen als auch den zeitlich befristeten, für ihre unermüdliche Mithilfe.

Volker Fischer

Acknowledgement

I would like to thank the following people and firms for their support and dedication in realizing this venture:

Richard Meier and the staff of his office in New York, especially Lisetta Koe, who managed the organisation of the venture with enormous care, and also Esther Kim and Elizabeth Lee;

all the manufacturers who have made contributions – Adrian Olabuenaga from Acme Studios, Dr. Alberto Alessi Anghini and Francesca Appiani from Alessi Spa, Arabia (here Stefan Ytterborn and Mia Hesselgren from Ytterborn & Fuentes and Denise Costantino from Designor, Inc.), Dan Baldinger and Katherine Wildt from Louis Baldinger & Sons, Inc., Carlo Valli and Marinella Formenti from Fusital (Valli & Valli), Rud. Ibach Sohn, Andrew Cogan and Peter Cogan from Knoll International, Jack Markuse from Markuse, Cleto Munari, Alessandro Munari and Valentina Nardi from Cleto Munari, Alan Buff from Reed & Barton, Patricia Marti from Steuben, John Longfellow and Mark Walters from Stow Davis and Nan Swid from Swid Powell;

the Frankfurt private bank Hauck & Aufhäuser for its financial involvement;

the transport firm Schenker Deutschland AG, Kelsterbach;

Axel Menges and Dorothea Duwe and their team for the excellent publication – the first about the museum to appear since several years;

and, finally, my collegues in the museum, both permanent and contract, for their tireless assistance.

Volker Fischer

Abbildungsnachweis / Sources of illustrations

Alessi (Aldo Ballo) 36.1
Peter Blundel Jones 11.5
Cleto Munari 54.2, 55.3
Uwe Dettmar 88.4, 88.5, 89.6, 89.7, 89.8, 89.9, 100.1, 102.4, 103.5, 104.6, 105.7 106.8, 107.9, 107.10, 108.11, 109.12, 109.13, 110.14, 111.15, 111.16. 112.17, 113.18, 114.19, 115.20, 115.21, 116.22, 116.23, 117.24, 118.25, 118.26, 119.27, 120.28, 121.29, 121.30, 122.31, 122.32, 123.33, 124.34, 125.35
Scott Frances 19.3
Fusital 28.14, 28.15, 28.16, 29.17, 29.18, 29.19, 29.20
Knoll International 15.4, 18.1, 18.2, 20.5, 20.6
Richard Meier & Partners 10.3, 19.4, 54.1, 83.1, 83.2, 92.1, 93.2, 93.3, 94.4, 95.5, 96.6, 97.7, 98.8, 99.9
Rudolf Nagel 101.2, 101.2
Bill Sharpe 22.8, 23.9, 24.10, 25.11
Steven Sloman 26.12, 27.13, 37.2, 38.3, 38.4, 39.5, 39.6, 40.7, 41.8, 42.9, 43.10, 44.11, 45.12, 45.13, 46.14, 46.15, 47.16, 47.17, 48.18, 48.19, 49.20, 49.21, 50.22, 50.23, 51.24, 51.25, 51.26, 56.4, 56.5, 57.6, 62.1, 62.2, 63.3, 63.4, 64.5, 64.6, 65.7, 65.8, 66.9, 67.10, 68.11, 68.12, 69.13, 70.14, 71.15, 71.16, 72.17, 72.18, 73.19, 73.20, 74.21, 74.22, 75.23, 76.24, 76.25, 77.26, 77.27, 78.28, 79.29, 80.30, 80.31, 81.32, 81.33
Ulli Steinmetz 21.7
Luca Vignelli 2
Vitra (Hans Hansen) 15.5

Gabriele Fahr-Becker, *Wiener Werkstätte*, Köln 1994 32.1, 33.4
Gilbert Frey, *The Modern Chair: 1850 to Today*, Teufen 1970 14.1, 15.3, 17.6
Heinz Geretsegger, Max Peintner, *Otto Wagner 1841–1918*, Salzburg 1964 10.4
Walter Gropius, Laszlo Moholy-Nagy, *Neue Arbeiten der Bauhaus-Werkstätten*, München 1925 (Bauhausbücher, 7) 17.7
Peter Noever, *Josef Hoffmann. Designer*, München 1992 14.2, 33.2, 33.3
Richard Meier. Museum für Kunsthandwerk Frankfurt am Main, Berlin 1985 (Ezra Stoller) 8.1, 9.2
Karin Thomas, *Bis heute. Stilgeschichte der bildenden Kunst im 20. Jahrhundert*, Köln 1971 61.8
Vladimir Tolstoi, *Art Decoratif Sovietique 1917 à 1937*, Paris 1989 34.5, 35.1, 58.2
Herta Wescher, *Die Geschichte der Collage*, Köln 1974 58.1, 59.3, 59.4, 60.5, 60.6, 61.7